WEAK
WITHOUT A
VICE

A collection of poetry & prose by
LAUREN RADEY

FOR THE DREAMERS, READERS,
LOVERS, DEEP THINKERS, POETS,
MUSICIANS AND ARTISTS
FAR AND WIDE
WHO HAVE CHALLENGED, INSPIRED,
AND NURTURED ME
ON THIS BEAUTIFUL,
TUMULTUOUS JOURNEY.

ALL MY LOVE.

I CAN'T HOLD
MY TONGUE
ANY LONGER,
SO I'LL SET IT FREE,
LET IT TELL YOU
EVERYTHING
YOU'VE EVER
DREAMED OF
HEARING.

mind control

allow me, tonight,
to escape your right brain
and travel elsewhere.

your corpus callosum invites me
to dance across
to your left side mind.

there, I'll render
your logic irrelevant, and trust —
you'll like it.

deliciously infiltrating your every synapse,
clouding your judgement,
implanting memories not yet made.

rewiring neural pathways,
thus, perceiving me in everything —
consciousness overtaken entirely.

spring fever

rain droplets gather on the windshield,
your hands resting on the steering wheel,
eyes downcast and focused on my thigh,
listening intently to the words that spill
so freely from my lips in your presence.

as you sip your coffee indulgently,
you tell me about your family,
and I can't help noticing the lines
around your eyes when you smile,
the way the light hits your hair.

you turn to me,
and the temperature in this car rises.
you see through my façade
to all the darkness and torment,
yet no part of you wants to run.

you reach for me with calloused hands,
cradling my face, fingertips tracing
my jaw as you draw in a breath
that takes mine away, falling
into the abyss of my embrace.

you and I belong somewhere
in the woods in a cabin by a stream,
where the frogs and the rain on the roof
and the headboard against the wall
are the only sounds at night.

we are kindred spirits
searching for silence
in a screaming world.

in the moonlight

meet me at the marina -
you bring the coffee,
and I'll buy the cigarettes.

the radio playing
some outlaw country song;
truck bed and blankets.

your leg against mine,
telling me what you were like
when you drank too much.
you look to the stars -
'what do you think
it all means?'

I could say it,
but it's hard to be cynical
in the moonlight,

and your fingertips
distract me when
they're drawing on my hand.
you hit me with
a long, slow kiss.

'this.'

in April

love left me in April.
I knew it was over
when she sauntered in
one night at 3 a.m.,
her hair all a mess,
merlot on her breath,
smelling like him.

she crawled into bed,
tucking those eternally cold feet
between mine,
razorblade fingernails
tracing my chest,
drunk lips pleading
'one last time'.

and I think
she pity-fucked me,
but I didn't mind.
when it comes to her,
I'll take what I can get.

I clung to that
gaunt little body
for dear life.
why did I let go?

why did she have to
leave me on the edge,
helpless and wanting?

why did she
have to get dressed
and take off without
any of her things again?
countless reminders
of what we were,
left strategically behind.

why did she
have to leave me
thinking of her, day and night,
fickle little bitch that she is,
coming and going
whenever the fuck
she pleases?

and I leave
the porch light on,
knowing she'll come
and make me come
again one day.

and I'll let her in.
and this time,
I swear I won't think
she's here to stay —
I swear I'll be ready
for her to leave me
lonely and desperate,

with everything
amiss like this
again.

lioness

there's a lioness in my heart —
it ain't Bukowski's bluebird.
she tries to claw her way out,
snarling and panting
and scampering around,
ravenous and ready
to kill anything that moves.

I don't have to chase
my prey — it comes to me.
men so trusting and naïve
believe I'm delicate and sweet.
I have them laying at my feet,
swallowing my lies —
then I eat them alive.

self-made grave

too self-involved to save me.
it was wrong to indulge you
when you said two wrongs
might make a right this time.
knew better, but you intrigued me.
played the charade till
it was real, began to feel.
and at least one of us fell into a well.
and I've always been fond
of drowning - what an ending.
bathtub glamour, car over bridge,
3 a.m. turbulent swim —
though last night, I was hell-bent
on dying by means of speed,
lead foot and engine revving,
155 km/h, laughing uncontrollably.
please, something kill me.
trying to feel anything but this
paralyzing numbness.
how about glass in the face,
brains on the pavement,
blood pooling rapidly?
what a fucking scene it would have been
to come upon — disarming.
who would read the eulogy?
would you even miss me?

or would you just fill
the ever-vacant space
with another pretty face?
some bubbly blonde twig,
with no desire to put you in your place,
eager for you to desecrate her face,
as I decay six feet deep
in my self-made grave.

devotion

These visions haunt my waking hours as love-struck ecstasy replaces rationality. We stand no chance and are destined for staggering eternities simultaneously. A rollercoaster fairy tale with an undetermined ending. A collection of fatalities and impossible realities. Tell me the odds of coming upon something that causes us to reevaluate our reckless habits, our hearts to flood with unconditional compassion.

Tell me how a jaded woman is reduced to wanting apprehension by the low melody of his voice at 2 a.m., imagining the gravitational pull of slow-moving hands. Tell me how a restless man falls headlong into pools of mirrored ink, his customary slew of words reduced to sighs and stutters, pausing carefully to think before uttering romantic proclamations and unintentional poetry. Tell me the beauty in a single moment, were we walking alongside this mystical river hand in hand.

Were we to pause and melt together, were fingers to rake through windblown hair, were eyes locked intimately and quivering lips whispering three words we ache each day to hear. If kisses lasted hours, if we could love even threads of darkness out of one another. If passion and consistency could convince scarred hearts to believe in something impenetrable and everlasting.

Call me a dreamer. Call me irrational, but I believe in something that surpasses all understanding. Call me late at night and confess your sins to me. Learn my mind until my body is yours to keep. Until I am the last thing you see before you drift off to sleep. Until you wake with my hair draped across your chest, drawing in a deep, easy breath, grounded by the heat of me. Until you see clearly what it is you've been missing. Until my devotion has you believing you deserve everything you seek.

sahara

how long will you roam these barren desert plains,
scaling dunes and descending slip face slacks,
vigilantly enduring the hostile hyperaridity
of the torrid climate I impose
upon those who choose to peruse me?

a suffocating simoom induced by saltating sand,
you devoutly withstand my blistering brutality.
gritty grains slip through tremulous hands
as you search tirelessly for my fabled oasis,
desiring only to drink endlessly from elusive streams.

throat parched and sanity dwindling,
heatstroke hallucinations propel scalded feet;
disoriented though miraculously inclined
to survive destructive proclivities —
you are a nomad destined to travel me.

and you see my Saharan expanse is only
the means to the end you seek in me;
for despite my inhospitable ergs and valleys,
the banks of my paradisiacal Nile
lie to the east — nearly within reach.

body language

my cyanotic lips may say,
'do not resuscitate',
but my body language
whispers otherwise.
any logical part of me
is overridden by
starry-eyed romanticism,
unwilling to let this
lustful apprehension die.

compress my chest.
crack these ribs wide open
all over again.
press your mouth to mine, and breathe
this hollow skeleton back to life.
I'd rather this ache,
this tender existence,
than to slip back into
blissful numbness.

autumn leaves

our eyes met in the autumn haze.
I lost myself within his maze.
he spoke no words yet said it all —
into his arms I soon would fall.

that night I lay beside the lake,
wondering how long it would take,
till shadows fell and footsteps came -
upon his parted lips, my name.

'come closer,' - words I couldn't say.
he seemed to hear me anyway.
lost within his fiery stare,
he ran a cold hand through my hair.

a twist of fate, a changing tide,
two hearts destined to collide.
the gentle sound of his guitar,
two voices singing in the dark.

we talked for hours that starlit night.
wrapped in his arms, the world was right.
his hungry lips drew mine apart.
he took my body and my heart.

tangled up, alive and spent;
I thought I'd never love again.
he promised me we'd find a way,
that I'd see him again one day.

but seasons pass and people change.
the cards of life are rearranged.
I hear his voice, a haunting sound —
when autumn leaves fall to the ground.

shotgun girl

midnight freeway
and a girl beside you,
her blonde hair wild,
tangling in the wind,
hand on your thigh.
she's smiling, always is.

as you drive, he and I
will drink on the porch,
stars glowing overhead,
smoke on our breath,
talking about things
you and I never did.

please…
don't let it come to this.

lingering

I could make a muse of him
much the same as I did
at this time last year,
but I know better.
his power was
immeasurable
for a time,
and quite frankly,
he's the reason
I'm here;
the reason
I wrote a book;
the reason I changed
the course of my entire life.
he never had a choice
in the matter,
and now we laugh
and have this relaxed,
platonic banter.
but sometimes —
sometimes
I glance at him,
remembering what he once did,
and all the things
I longed to then,
but never got the chance to.

and I think
there's an intrigue
he feels too —
perhaps now
more than ever.
but he's wise,
and won't disrupt
the course of his life
for an unpredictable
catastrophe like me.
and it's fine,
because admittedly,
I'm over it.
still, I'll never forget
the way it felt
to be under his spell,
tangled in his web,
to have his name lingering
with the raspberry sour
on my breath.

worst case

worst case scenario,
you leave
in the morning
with the scent of me
lingering
in your beard,
claw marks
etched into your back,
and a 'when
will I see you again',
silently strangled
in your throat.

worst case scenario,
my pillow smells
like your cologne,
my skin is raw from
the relentless impact
of your palm,
my lips are bitten,
my legs are still
aftershock quivering,

and I've finally
gotten you
out of my system.

lately

lately, I've been drinking whiskey
and counting up the men who miss me,
but I've long since run out of fingers;
shame the way the thought of me lingers.

and I like it this way, if I'm truthful.
I'll keep ripping out hearts while I'm youthful.
strangling my demons with medication,
pills and smoke and lustful fixation.

I can't seem to mend the gaping wound.
no amount of distraction will do.
how will I right the wrongs of my past,
and when the hell will anything last?

I have been beaten down so many times;
once a pitiful victim of various crimes,
and in my refusal to break again,
I began to use my body as a weapon.

I am not a good woman at heart.
deception and trickery, to me, are an art.
beneath my desire for their singular lust
is a blatant refusal to give my trust.

therapy costs a pretty penny,
so I drown myself in Wiser's and Henny,
and raise a glass to all the rest
who'll try to thaw the block of ice in my chest.

hopscotch

settle down, settle down.
he is not here to replace
the feeling that's begun
to fizzle and fade.
playing hopscotch,
jumping these men
in a figurative sense,
while indulging in a visual
of everything literal,
is not going to fill
the canyon-like void
that is your longing
for 'it all'.
you may never find
the one with a tongue
that stimulates both
your body and mind —
right there,
but certainly,
it will not be
for lack of trying.

these hands

I make you sweat
with words alone —

imagine
what
these
hands
would
do.

skeletons

paint crumbles, flutters to the floor,
trembling fingers tracing bare walls,
floorboards creaking eerily
under bare, ivory feet,
pausing in the hall to gaze
in a dilapidated mirror —
a ghostly reflection staring back.
hollow heart palpitating,
shrouded in shimmering black.
dark shadows under midnight eyes,
lips blood-red and unsmiling,
hair damp and unruly.
a ghastly shell of a woman
with a closet full of skeletons,
a basement full of bodies,
October wind howling ominously,
chandelier flickering cryptically.
sinking into a rickety kitchen chair,
sipping another evil concoction.
alone but never lonely —
these ghosts forever haunting.

ashes

get out of the house.
buy an urn.
fill it with the ashes of us.
close the lid.
cry a little.
set it on the mantle.
look at it awhile.
pour yourself a drink.
rest your spinning head.
let it be dead.

I write to you

I write today if only to convey a lack of remorse for what I do. An age-old story uttered anew. Listless limbs and lead garments causing cyanotic spluttering below a whirling surface. Doubting purpose, the unspoken pursuit of wayward dreams deemed worthless.

I know it all too well. Senseless souls who pray for rain in hell, who have crawled over coals dragging broken femurs, fragility masked by cold demeanours, still alive but barely, seeking solace yet tasting it rarely. Hearts weak from lovers past, egos and sternums contused, bruised, eager flesh defiled and used, abused as the audience stares, amused.

Yet oceanic eyes utter wordless assurances of equal endurance, and I find myself not only stealing the show, but staging an elaborate heist to claim the passionate fortune in the vault of heart and mind. The keys not hanging from a ring, but rather unconventional in their mechanism. Words softly sung as you drift off to dream, shared visions of coastal footprints and cabin-side streams, morning coffee, no sugar, no cream.

And despite our habitual dualism, realities converge in compromising fashion. The bloodletting oddly effective as we heal from the shattering calamity of prior crashes.

Regarding burn marks and lashes with understanding, faulty parachutes landing with magnificent force — yet not enough to kill. Battered and bandaged, laughter infectious, recounting the thrill.

Despite fearing the dark, I immerse myself in it. Hands stained by soot and ink, I sit cross-legged beneath the moon to think of you and the warmth of your glow, as you shine through the cracks of a boarded-up window.

barstool chemistry

we were blatant barstool chemistry,
legs intertwined accidentally,
pale ale foam lingering
on smirking lips, leaning in,
a blaring music-induced excuse
to hover recklessly on the precipice
of a door-rattling, palm-over-lips 'yes'.

we were the only two in a buzzing room,
kinky poems scrawled on bar napkins,
wandering hands and palpable tension,
neon light gleaming in ravenous eyes,
bodies falling victim to an intricate rhythm,
hop-laced breath erratic as we danced,
minds racing to a 2 a.m. hotel bed.

unchain me

I could be an affliction. An addiction, if you let me.

If you met me under flickering streetlight. If we slow danced in the moonlight. If August firelight reflected in black eyes, revealing an appetite for burning demise. If cicadas were records and stars were candlelight. If we ran for the sand beach, only to be swept from our feet by the waves and the wanting and the sunset breeze.

And if I'm tongue-tied, unwind me. If I tear through your skin, bind me. If I'm swallowed by the night, find me, and bring me back from the depths of my fantasies, and ground me in the startling uncertainty of reality. Fill me with every inch of you I need, plant the seed of carnal greed in my womb and exhume these wayward dreams from their tomb.

Overcome me. Demand that I plead, and I'll teach you how to bleed in a way you never dreamed you could. Choke me out. Leave me breathless. Beating hearts restless.

Claim my mind as your property by worshipping this broken body, tear down every crumbling city within me, and rebuild me, gild me, possess me, and press me to your lips, and unchain me with your hips, and damage me and bandage me and play these long-untouched keys, and please – don't stop.

an apology

If you're reading this, I'm sorry.

I'm sorry you were the only person I saw in the room. That I was drawn to you. That I got in that car with you. That I heard the way you spoke to someone vulnerable and fell for your kindness. That I was allowed to be fragile around you. That you listened. That you asked me questions. That you laughed at my dark jokes and read my poetry. That despite conversations about our significant others, I was picturing you with me.

I'm sorry I allowed attraction to border on obsession. That you became the muse for nearly everything I was writing. That I kept trying. That I misinterpreted our interactions as being more than platonic. That I believed there might be a thread of interest on your side. That I became jittery when in a room with you. That my tongue froze in my mouth when I tried to speak to you. That I was blind to your faults. That I was honest with you. That I couldn't let go even after I told you I wanted you. That your presence continued to fuel me. That I got high on you knowing exactly what I was thinking.

I'm sorry for the tension. For the glances that never meant anything. For that night when I was drinking. For putting you in that position. For hugging you in the kitchen.

For writing that last poem. For being accusatory and angry. For what led to you distancing yourself from me, as much as it has helped me.

I'm sorry it couldn't be easy. That we couldn't just be friends from the beginning. That I saw in you something I'd always been missing and wanted you to fill my empty spaces. I'm sorry I can't erase this. I'm sorry I got in that car. I'm sorry I went too far.

men at work

I'm a naughty oddity.

the men at work
drop in to talk to me,
and we shoot the shit
till one of us becomes restless,
(usually him),
strolling merrily away,
as if he won't be back
later in the day
with a clever new thing to say.

indirectly requesting
my cellphone number,
casually mentioning coffee,
asking if I like it.
no shit, I have a full cup
right here on my desk.

trying with much effort
to feign innocence.
and it's all the same —
I shouldn't complain
that they're lining up
out there for me.

but God,
they've got
no fucking game,
and they're always far too busy
staring at me from behind
to give a flying fuck
what's going on
inside my mind.

toothpaste

I was always reckless
with the toothpaste tube —
left it crinkled and warped,
and like clockwork he would
straighten the kinks,
squeeze it all to the end,
and lay it back down
for me to wreck again.

we used to smile at
reflections in the mirror -
I'd be wrapped in a towel,
and he'd be in his underwear.
I would brush my teeth
hurriedly, viciously,
and he would take his time;
let me spit first.
mint flavour lingering
between morning molars,
brushing my tongue and
accidentally gagging myself —
he would laugh, and I'd slap him.

I hope he finds someone
who treats the tube
and his heart with more care.

dead flowers

wicked dreams bring forth
whispered pleas from lips
that snap shut, twitch guiltily,
night-time paralysis defied.

eyes flutter open,
conscious of mistakes.
pulsing arteries lessen their pace,
reassured; he's still asleep.

one assaults me like the plague,
the other stirs from peaceful slumber —
drapes a heavy arm around me,
drifting back to honest places.

skin, damp with sweat sings beneath
his touch, languid bodies intertwine.
no sense plucking petals from daisies —
he loves me.

yet I dream of something
so overwhelming...
the ghost of love not-given;
a penniless stargazer.

ending the masquerade,
ripping my body apart
with my love letters
as I try to rest my weary eyes.

back blistering on beach sand,
body bowing on a grand piano,
lips moving faster
than the east-bound train we ride on.

not something I can't have,
but something I shouldn't.
I'm tired of watering a flower
that's already dead.

older man

another older man
has my attention by the neck,
choking with a vice-like grip
till it's blue in the face,
and finally turned on —
(it takes a lot).

Daddy Issues receives the award
for Most Plausible Explanation.
the crowd applauds half-heartedly,
all young, dumb and pretty
with stricken expressions.

I tell myself it's experience
that draws me in.
silver hair and expert hands,
delicate wrinkles when he smiles,
fierce hazel eyes
brimming with wisdom.

it's a mixed drink of reasons —
absent father syndrome,
lack of stability,
attraction to maturity,
and a splash of self-sabotage.

succeeding in seducing him
is the fix for this addiction.
the attraction wanes instantly
when I get him underneath me.
he falls for me deeply;
I wonder what I've done.

the part of me that daydreams
of wedding vows and babies
emerges, regurgitates the offer
to come to Christmas dinner
with his twenty-year old daughter.

this isn't going to work.
he's hurt and I'm numb.
they say 'find a man your age',
but I couldn't care less —
I'll play this game again
with another older man.

the moth and the spider

you wove a web —
delicate, translucent,
softly shimmering
in the fading light.
how clumsy of me,
how naïve
to fly toward you,
to let this
insatiable curiosity
get the best of me.
wings now tangled
in your threads,
I writhe in place,
awaiting
your approach.
but instead,
you keep me
at arm's length
as you reinforce
this maze of yours,
taking pleasure
in my presence,
taunting me
with your indifference,
as I wait in agony
to be eaten alive.

the madness

don't write for him.
don't let words
become stanzas
that mirror
his desires.
he does not know
your fire.
he can't appreciate
a force of nature.
and so, you are trying
to tame yourself
on his account,
but you are
much more powerful
than the way
he grips you.
a braver man
will be addicted
to the madness in you.

sick serenade

I saw you tonight,
leaning up against the bar.
a hundred strangers turned to stare
as my glass hit the floor —
a sea of gin and crystal
beneath my stilettos.
'honey, you look pale.'
feverishly scanning the faces,
but I'm hallucinating again.

you keep yourself at such a distance —
not as impulsive as you claim to be.
you give me time
while more melts away.
if you came for me,
I'd change —
become a slave to my darkest desires,
drop the façade
like some kind of reckless hero.

we'd walk these city streets at night
taking shots at every bar,
and I'd kiss another man
just to make you want to fight,
lead me back to your place,
make me pay for my transgressions.

you'd pin me to the wall,
your mouth on my neck;
sweet, merciless punishment.
we'd be lying spent in your bed,
heating the room with candles,
smoking cigarettes and singing Sinatra —
a moonlight serenade.

living on simple dreams
and the taste of your kiss,
you'd free my soul from its bindings,
and I'd show you how it feels
to really be loved.

until then,
keep me somewhere in your heart,
let me haunt and inspire you
as much as you do me.
you're my sweet illusion,
my angel without wings,

my only regret —

that is, unless,
you find me.

you and my imagination

and still, despite
the fortitude it took
to quell my desire for you,
you reach for me furiously
in wayward morning dreams
and grip my throat, screaming.
surveying me in empty hallways,
drawn to me behind thin doors;
I am spread across your desk,
papers scattering, spiralling
to the floor as I grip the wood edges
for leverage as your mouth
opens mine, tongue limp,
and my teeth sink into your lip,
biting hard till you react —
kissing me feverishly.
your hands firmly grip
my wrists, bruising me;
the feral rhythm of you
within me causing me
to cry out loudly.
your eyes flash, and your palm
cups my mouth harshly,
though you quickly forget
about silencing me
as I move your hand enough

to slide two of your fingers
deep into my mouth,
and I don't choke
even as they reach
the back of my throat.
and I watch you
fall apart above me,
come undone for me,
my name on your lips;
a willing slave to me.
but I wake alone,
tense and aching,
remembering
you're far more level
in reality than you are
in these pervasive fantasies.
and fuck, I hate
the naughty things
you and my imagination do to me.
you never came to me,
or for me, regrettably,
but you won't leave me,
and perhaps you would —
if only the thought of you
didn't feel so fucking good.

broody man

broody man
with heavy eyelids —
in need of a haircut
and a week of sleep,
shuffling your feet,
jittery all day,
benzos and caffeine.
reading, writing,
walking, unlocking
the apartment at night,
filling it with smoke,
slouched over
in that second-hand chair,
pen between your teeth,
wrestling with words
till your head hurts.
ibuprofen and Heineken,
checking her Instagram,
wishing you spoke
her body language,
imagining her legs
around your waist — Christ.
writing a poem she'll 'like',
but does she really?
how do you tell her...
they're all about her?

all bad

we can't keep this up.
I've had enough of this.
waiting for a sign that says
anything but 'stop'.

if I scream into the void all night,
you won't hear me;
dawdling around cluelessly
with your headphones on.

it's fruitless being hot for you
whilst my feet fucking freeze.
hell knows he should have
more of me than my apathy.

congrats - you possessed me,
but you can't have the rest of me,
you won't get the best of me,
'cause there isn't any left in me, baby.

I'm all bad.

rock and roll

I was jazz music
on a Friday night
when you wanted
to rock and roll.

you were suave, dressed in black,
heard us playing on the sidewalk,
stopped in your tracks;
bustling crowd pushing past.

mesmerized, you ducked inside,
took the last seat at the bar,
watched me from afar;
fingers flying over piano keys.

the band and I had a knack
for firing up a crowd —
had you dancing in your seat
to that saxophone drawl.

after the final act,
I slipped off the stage,
beads of sweat on my face,
euphoric as I looked your way.

you romanced me,
arm draped around me.
I leaned in to tell stories,
and you begged to hear more from me.

ensnared by wit and charm
and your mischievous eyes,
the ring on your left hand
was hardly a surprise.

we danced until you left me
with a top-shelf whiskey kiss,
alone beneath the neon light
as you vanished in the night.

you walked the mile home
with my body on your mind,
kissed your naïve girl awake,
made love to her all night.

and in the background,
the radio played
rock and roll.

tension and whiskey

rampant flames lick timber,
painting irises maniacally
in a darkened room as we fail
to drown tension in whiskey.

please don't treat me nicely.

languid limbs pinned
to the hearth beneath you,
writhing as you drink in
every molten drop of me.

a dream

I had a dream
you poured your heart out
and told me everything
you'd been afraid
to imagine with me.

I had a dream
there was unread poetry
caged in notebooks,
never unleashed,
until you bared it all to me.

I had a dream
you took a chance on us,
on me, and your intention
was to one day be
my everything.

I had a dream,
and I'm awake now,
breathless and aching,
bleeding heart craving
your loyalty.

I had a dream,
a lapse in consciousness,
and conjured up vivid images
and visceral pangs
of what will never be.

I had a dream —
and it was far from reality.

instant gratification

battling this monogamous mind,
gently reminding it it's alright
to look, taste, touch,
convincing it that even if
it gets caught on someone —
they are not similarly set on me,
and it will only be detrimental
if I fixate once again
on something I created
inside my head.

it's a fine line
using a single person
for poetic inspiration when
you're wishing they were silencing
your endless verse with their lips.

but if it isn't real yet,
it begs the question of whether
it ever would be.

the lines drawn between us
will simultaneously keep him
from falling or withdrawing,
and limbo doesn't feel nice,

so I swiped right last night
only to match with a man
similarly distant;
less interested in my intellect,
more fixated on the thought
of my legs wrapped around his neck.

and I don't hate the thought of it,
but he is yet another breathing 'maybe'
I could carry on baiting
for months on end,
just often enough to remind him
of what he might get
in a moment of weakness,
by way of a drunk text.

so easy to get my hands on
even a Greek god like him,
because we're both easy
under the right circumstances.

and I pretend not to complicate it,
but in all honesty, I'm not sure
how many more times
I can give away my body
so carelessly

with the pitiful hope
they'll want to hold on to me,
and I to them,
that we'll finally find that evenness
I've never experienced —
the kind where neither lover
has the upper hand,
where both feel passionately
and purely and equally.

I have to wonder what it's like,
because this instant gratification
leaves my heart weak and empty,
and while we all long to be wanted,
I deserve more respect
than I've ever given myself
or any of them.

remember together

10:04 p.m., a double bed with a wrought iron frame, tucked away amidst a slew of pillows, buried in blankets, pondering this lasting loneliness. And I think of you - whoever you are. I long for you here, distracting me from this miserable situation; from the ways I've regressed in my living since leaving the comfortable life I slaved for years to create.

I imagine you behind me in this bed, my head against your chest, my hair spilling over your arm. Gazing up at you as you read a passage from some obscure poetry book, my hand gripping the back of your neck and pulling your mouth to mine, interrupting your seamless stream of words, and loving how they feel against my lips in the moments before you are too distracted by my kiss to finish your sentence.

Unapologetic hands tearing off t-shirts and sweatpants, our fingers interlaced, face to face, hungry bodies entirely in sync. Endeavoring to keep quiet so my roommates won't hear us this time. Your mouth on my ear saying, 'you're mine'. And I am, and I want to shout it to everyone on earth who ever tried to claim me. I may be more independent than anyone you've ever met, but fuck, if I don't love the idea of being possessed.

Of giving myself entirely to you. Is that not what I live for? Is it ever the wrong thing to do?

I couldn't care less about the possibility of being ruined by you. I know I would do this all over with you regardless. I would take minutes of your breath on my neck over a lifetime of loneliness. I would rip the stars from the heavens and put them in my eyes just to show you what it is you do. This pull you have on me.

The way I can be standing alone in the kitchen washing dishes and am suddenly engulfed in a vivid daydream of you behind me, your arms locked around my waist, your mouth warm on the nape of my neck, creating a wanting chill that travels up my spine, heat rising between my thighs, my body melting perfectly to yours, moulded to the shape of you, one with you, a flush colouring my cheeks, forgetting to breathe, smiling indulgently and feeling your lips curl against my skin as we remember together what happiness is. Saying that I want you is an understatement. I would kill or be killed for just a taste of you.

> If only you knew me, and I you.

breathe

these are the good days —
working the late shift
all week and weekend,
counting pennies
to pay the rent.
finding spare seconds
to curl up on the couch
with the windows
and my eyes half-shut,
bathing in silence.

so busy I'm dizzy all the time.
trying to occupy my mind,
but it still finds
a way to ruin me...
fucking anxiety.

guess I should be glad
I haven't broken down yet
the way I did last year.
I was half dead then,
sleeping sixteen hours a day,
sobbing and shaken
and desperate for a change
I had no energy to make.

(this paralyzing fear
of things staying the same
will be the death of me.)
I'm scared of everything,
like your consistency.
tension every time
there are eyes on me,
trembling hands, weak knees,
voice cracking when I speak.

in my head,
they all see
right through me.
they find pleasure
in how broken I am.

they are dreaming
up ways to
rip me apart.

I need to breathe,
I know,
and slow
this frantic heart.

I need to mend
these wounds,
but where the fuck
do I start?

everything

I am not much to you,
though perhaps one day,
there will be a book
on your coffee table
with my name on its spine,
and you will fold over
a page here,
a page there —
whatever.

I am something
for you to read,
something pretty
to look at,
maybe,
interesting,
undoubtedly,
but I am just your
'good morning'
in the hall,
a once-over,
a fleeting smile,

and you,

are

e
v
e
r
y
t
h
i
n
g
.

careless

is it hot in here,
or is it our proximity?
your lips carelessly near
as you whisper in my ear.
inches closer and I'd feel
the heat of your exhale.
needing more of you,
(tell me anything).
the crowd around us
vanishing,
voices fading,
aching, as once again,
you leave me
starving.

sometime in September

we were sprawled out on your bed
with all the windows open,
chain-smoking in our underwear
sometime in September.
I kissed you, teeth tightening
around your bottom lip,
while you grinned,
called me the devil,
sprung up to put another record on,
stretched, muscles taut,
searching for
the perfect album
while I watched
the flexion of your forearms,
the distension of your veins,
and the way you were
a living, breathing heartache.
beside me
on the bedside table
was a half-drunk bottle of wine.
I downed a quarter of it
as that song started to play,
and you crawled up
from the foot of the bed,
lay there next to me,
your leg draped over me,

your fingers in my hair.
and we sang
until the lyrics
had their way with me
and tears filled my eyes.
you just smiled,
put your cigarette
between my lips.
I took a long, helpless breath,
and in that moment
your eyes could talk and they said,
'I don't know you, but I want to,'
with strange sincerity.
maybe it was just the wine
that got me crying,
but when I covered my face,
you lifted my hands,
held them in yours
and told me not to apologize
for feeling so much.
and those words left me
brimming with an uncommon lust -
the kind that allows you
to open yourself
without conditions,
the kind that leaves chills

along your jaw, on your neck,
the kind that begs you
to let it all out
as it buries its face
in that delicate place,
turns you into
a dominant creature
and a slave.
it had you underneath me,
soft light flickering
in your awestruck eyes.
it had me powerful,
arching backward,
every demon exorcised -
one with you and the night.
and you held me
even after
I stopped trembling.
and you took me
again and again,
all the ways
I longed to be taken.
and for that time, at least,
I was alive and free,
showing myself,
in all my destructive glory

to someone
who truly saw me.
and if that isn't living,
I don't know what is.

as you wish

loving you seems unwise,
until we have an oxytocin-induced excuse
for those three tantalizing words
that our mouths long to spill meaningfully,
to murmur over and over
as our bodies quiver and quake together.

and I need only the wordless promise of your lips,
the harsh hypnosis of your hips,
before I pledge my allegiance to only you —
my heart torn from intercostal space
and placed in your waiting palms
to do with as you wish.

the devil herself

This is different, yet no different than anything that ever has been. I am captivated, yet still conscious of the inevitable damage. I walk in already planning my exit.

The collision of two broken souls creates the brightest of fireworks. Lived experience, incomparable passion, a ridiculous expectation of some ever-unattainable perfection.

If I tell you that you have me, I am lying. No one does. No one has. No one can. You'll see it as a challenge. Good luck to you, then.

I am a monster in soft, delicate skin. I draw you in. I am heaven and sin simultaneously. I am incredibly good at playing on your every want and need. I am the devil herself. Do you hear me? Run away. I may say I want you to stay till the end, but I am lying.

That's the price of being brutally broken. The price of once being so utterly convinced of my own worthlessness that I deny anyone who ever tries. I wanted to die. I wished for the end of my existence, but was too weak to complete the deed. And so, I live. And I morphed from that pathetic wreck into this. This.

The men who shunned me once come running. Wanting.

I am a magnet, and you are naïve. Blinded by beauty, unaware of what I am. Come closer so that I might cut you deep. I will manipulate you. I will do every single thing you've ever wanted a woman to do. I will tell you I love you, my breath warm on your ear.

Don't believe it. I don't even love myself. I am a walking defence mechanism. I am hell disguised as a woman. I am a collection of beatings, desirous only for revenge, and I prefer to unleash this anger on men.

I was born unwanted. What a sick turn of events to now be wanted desperately by many. You are feeding the insatiable void in me. I will drown my insecurity in your interest, your compliments and promises. I will spellbind you with my honesty. I will show you every part of me, except that one little glitch. The shut-off switch. I will be the best high you've had until it ends. It ends. It ends.

I am a monster in soft, delicate skin. I will destroy your entire life and leave you standing stunned in the ashes as I sidle off, never once looking back. I will care about you like no one ever has until I couldn't care less. I am the devil herself. You will believe you have me until it ends. It ends. It ends.

they call it falling

They call it falling, but I've not lost my balance, and I am not flailing or wailing or fearing a colossal crash onto pavement, a concussion or fracture or hemorrhage.

They call it falling, but when he lifts me in his arms I am held in place, gripping handfuls of unruly hair. His lips are light on my neck and my legs are locked firmly around his waist and he carries me to bed, spreads me gently atop the covers, and I am pulling him close and our bodies are mirrors and my hands are relentless as they learn his intricacies, and he sighs deeply against my mouth, the faint aroma of beer and smoke hanging in the air with our desire — and I am wholly intoxicated.

They call it falling, but I am far from powerless. I see the longing in his eyes when he gazes up at me. I hear it in the curses that escape his wanting mouth as our bodies move in startling synchrony. In his breathlessness. In the way he meets my curiosity with unabashed honesty. His eyes hold intense sincerity and when he smiles at me, I feel myself spinning - but I sense already that when I find myself dizzy, he'll be there waiting to hold me steady.

They call it falling, and perhaps I am. Tasting and craving so much more of him. Before I close my eyes to succumb to his inevitable gravity, I see his arms open and ready to catch me.

blue smoke

neon lights and blue smoke,
self-deprecating train wreck joke,
your head tilting back
like a 5 o'clock glass,
eyes crinkling at the sides.
and your style, your smile,
have me borderline performing,
fingertips light on your hand,
stealing your attention and pen,
my teeth grazing the tip slowly.
watching you watch me think,
taking a long, drawn-out drink
from a beat-up pint glass
as I scribble euphemisms
all over red-plated pages.
and you lean in to read
the open book and I —
dying to be vandalized.

harsh reality

My stomach heaves, and the cramps cripple me. And I am in a housecoat that's supposed to be sexy, and my face is flushed and blotchy, and my hair is wet from the bath that didn't help me, and I am curled in the fetal position as I listen to the soothing sound of a beautiful woman reading poetry, and it makes me feel if only a little less lonely. Later on, I'll switch on 'Friends' for company.

And I am writhing, but every movement is a hundred knives in my bloated belly, and the ache in my back is overwhelming. And all I have are fantasies of someone here to comfort me. An image of him, admittedly. I can almost feel him behind me, arms so naturally melting around me, his face buried in my hair as his hands move gently over swollen skin. I imagine him slipping off to put the kettle on and make tea, and the transfer of a steaming mug to me, and his eyes, kind and adoring. I imagine him distracting me with bad jokes and mischievous stories as I brace myself laughing when it hurts too much.

I imagine his touch again and get tangled in the memory of when he was sound asleep next to me. Reminiscing about how I lay there after he'd taken me, face in the pillow smirking dazedly.

How, then, his skillful hands began to work the knots from my back wordlessly.

Sleepy lips on my forehead rendering me needed, only to then be discarded, tossed aside like something easy to find within a matter of days. I can't count the ways he had me believing he'd be around in moments like this. But the harsh reality is, he isn't.

He didn't see me long enough to understand he ought to keep his hands on this tanned skin, hair blowing in the wind in the passenger's seat of his beat-up pickup truck, homemade dinner and beer in the fridge, head on his shoulder, scary movie in the darkness, intoxicating, slow drawn-out kiss, late-night temptation, giving in, stay the night, morning light streaming through the gaps in the curtains, wild-haired temptress leaving him cursing and breathless.

If he couldn't tie himself to that, then God knows he wouldn't have held on for this. Vulnerable and weak with everything amiss. And though the fleeting high he elicited felt better than the rest, I don't deserve less than the kind of man who can convince me of my beauty when I'm only a mess.

bloom

as overcast April skies
whisper of rainstorms,
we are blissfully oblivious,
warm and tightly wound
on a picnic blanket island,
in a sea of sweet, lush grass,
raspberry wine on our breath,
utterly transfixed and drunk
on this blossoming incipient love.

we emerge from the earth anew,
vibrant green chutes
fragile and tender together,
and my hands are the weather,
the balance you crave,
the nourishing rain
and sunlight alike that
ignite and incite the unfurling
of delicate wildflower petals.

in the throes of ethereal bliss,
our shared breath drowns
the harmonious choir
of sparrows and finches -
they who flit vivaciously
from ground to budding tree,

gathering twigs with haste,
fashioning intricate castles
to shelter their nestlings.

raindrops moisten ivory skin,
falling fast with intention.
pausing to gaze up at them,
our eyelashes flutter, heavy.
wet droplets stream over lips
that curl into knowing smiles.
you pull me in again,
and my pounding heart
can't help but to bloom for you.

safe word stop sign

I liked to be choked
a hell of a lot more
when I wasn't taking
this collection
of antidepressants.

a lover's eyes
searching mine for
a safe word stop sign,
as I dared him to hold
my throat tighter still.

I was suicidal,
numb as hell,
and losing breath,
lightheadedness,
were sensations
I could still be
forced to feel.

I always tried to measure
a man's passion,

and the results of my various tests
left me grim
and disappointed.

but if he'd held on
till it killed me,
I'd have finally
been cold
and satisfied.

these days I crave
a firm hand,
attentive lips,
a slow, sensual
crescendo of bliss.

but if I digress,
remember this -

when I say
more,
harder,
yes,

I don't have
a fucking limit.

chasing ghosts

I have this recurring dream, and it wakes me again and again just before dawn, shivering in bed and drenched in cold sweat.

When I close my eyes at night, I see you on a busy sidewalk in the city. You smile at me briefly with that lonely look in your eyes, and without a word you turn and walk into a faceless crowd.

With a heart full of questions, I call out to you, but you do not hear me, or perhaps you do and just continue on your way. (Which is it? The question plagues my mind even after I wake.)

I chase you in a panicked state, struggling through the masses, eyes fixed on your back as you press on further still out of my grasp. I try in vain to break through, fighting the sullen, slow-moving, barely-breathing bodies that close in around me, never allowing me past.

We walk for hours like this, and when the crowd finally disperses and the paved road turns to dirt, you remain there just ahead.

You roll your shoulders, stretch your arms, and run a hand through your sandy hair. My breath comes in rasps, and I am brimming with hope, needing nothing else on earth but to see the glow of sunlight once more on your face.

We march on till the sun finally sets, the sky painted vibrant shades of coral, peach, and red. There is sand beneath my feet, and once again we stand on an endless beach. You pull your shirt overhead and toss it aside, running straight for the tide.

A familiar chill creeps up my spine. I try to scream, but I have no voice. My feet reach the edge of the frigid sea and I collapse in the shallow, trembling.

You wade deeper and deeper until you disappear beneath a massive wave, and I know the ocean has swallowed you again.

This is when I wake, cold as your corpse with saltwater tears streaming down my face.

be the rain

you be the rain, baby,
and I'll be the tin roof.
pour down on me
from a grey July sky.
we both know this ain't
a song for the lonely,
when you're all-night
falling for me.
don't slow your pace.
trace my architecture.
learn me
drop by drop.
drench me,
quench me,
make love to me.
the sound we make
when we're together
is one poets and lovers
can't forget to remember.

over easy

you like your eggs
the way you like your women —
a little messy.

yellow smeared on
a white plate like paint,
buttered toast drowning
in yolk before
you lift it, sopping,
to your mouth —
hungry,
salivating.

early morning,
hair like Medusa,
bare legs dangling
from the countertop,
arms wrapped
around your neck,
warm, wet,
needing to be
devoured
like breakfast.
but I won't stay.

I'm only here
for sex and eggs,
and if you want
more from me,
baby,
we'll be over —
easy.

bleeding out

Men are the best band-aids until they're ripped off, and the skin goes with them, and the wound is still open, and it's bleeding — wait — I'm hemorrhaging, I'm slumped in a pool of scarlet on the floor, my pulse is plummeting, my lips are fading to blue and then and then...

Just in time, there's a glimmer of something - enough that my ambivalent floating soul manages to resuscitate my mangled body, and she is stroking my hair, and she's all 'it's okay, honey,' and she bathes me and scrubs the blood from the floor and fills the gashes with fresh packing and tapes them shut again. And she points to him, smiling.

And he becomes an obsession, and I am a racecar on love's speedway and his mouth is agape and I'm pedal to the floor long before they lower the flag. And I drive too fast, and sometimes they try to keep up, but they crash in their first lap, and I'm white-knuckled circling around the track gazing at their charred remains. Why doesn't anyone drive like me? Am I a maniac? Don't answer that.

I'm bleeding out again.

precipice

Chain-smoking cigarettes, huddled on the precipice, sparring with depressive feelings, ignoring any healing I've managed these past years. Damage and fears overwhelm my senses, render me spent and senseless as I reach with leaden arms for something to hold, and I'm told in a message that I am not alone, "Call me on the phone baby, I'll make you smile".

But in these trials, I allow myself to sink and spiral if only to remember the painful sensation that was my reality before the medication. Yet despite the tragedy that looms above me, in time I find myself dialling if only to fall into the depths of your addictive drawl. Curled in bed, eyes closed, surrendering to your gentle persuasion, balancing my equation with stories so ridiculous I can't help but to grin.

Soon breathless with laughter and transported elsewhere, to a dimly lit bedroom where I am similarly curled but around you, and your fingers trace over my arms, entirely out of harm's way if only for a day as your words echo against the walls, and my guard in its entirety falls.

Imagine my waking kiss, imagine feeling like this on a daily basis. Hush, and don't utter a word of it.

Be my summer secret that lasts fifty more. Let them whisper and wonder where we are as we hide away in the shelter of this apartment on the second floor, windows open wide, the birds outside singing ecstatically as you love me ruthlessly and I respond emphatically.

Hours later draw a scalding bath for me, sit on the floor next to me and read poetry as I slip beneath the bubbles, for once not wanting to remain beneath the surface forever. Together for days in ways that need not be explained. Piano keys played and vibrato voice haunting, cooking breakfast in your t-shirt as you dance and make coffee, simple pleasures and otherworldly musings alike, venturing out in the dark of night.

Chain-smoking cigarettes, huddled on the precipice. Your arm draped around me as you ramble about the galaxies. And if we happen to fall off the edge, it doesn't matter much. At least I'll have died having felt your touch.

in love with a poet

whatever you do,
don't fall in love
with a poet.

she will
break herself,
then you.

(her creativity
is fed by misery.)

no matter
what you give her,
she will never
be satiated.

her imagination
runs wilder
than the falls.

she plays it off,
but knows exactly
what she does.

she sinks so deep,
she starts to drown.

and when you try
in vain to save her,
she'll flail around,
cling to you —

and you'll lose
your breath too.

you say you'll stay
even if it kills you,
but you ought to think
of where that'll get you.

NEVER

funny how
the loyalty
I crave
in a man
annoys me
when I'm not
the one
receiving it.

all of you ought
to love me,
and only me.
(no one else.)

meanwhile,
I should be
free to love
whoever
my heart
(never)
desires.

THIS FEELING

I didn't think it would feel like this
when I talked about lightness.
I imagined emotionally intense,
but I never pictured myself
dancing around the kitchen
on a Tuesday night at dusk
with a wooden spoon microphone,
waiting for my phone to buzz,
waiting on another glimpse
of that wide, easy smile,
wild hair trapped beneath a ball cap,
kind eyes framed with laugh lines,
tanned skin, a drink in his hand,
conversations growing longer
with every rapidly-typed reply,
cheeks hurting while reading
every thought-out line he writes.
his silly jokes and singular interest,
the way he's making plans for us
even though we've yet to touch...
I don't remember the last time
I smiled quite this much,
and I'm trying not to fall too quickly,
but there's something
about this feeling.

the cynic

I scintillate with cyclical cynicism.
you tell me I'm lovely repetitively.
unfortunately, affirmations
rife with untried kindness
have never quite done it for me.
come morning you'll find
I greet the mirror with
'hey, stupid bitch,'
and I get along just fine.
words and promises die trying.
and let's face it,
you're more attractive when
you're long-winded and lying.
we'll be married at six
and divorced by nine.

spiders

the words I whisper in my sleep
are a darkened path leading to your apartment.
you elude me, but each night I draw closer,
and one day I will find the place
where the streetlight glimmers in your eyes
and the cold rain is imperceptible on my skin.
as I blindly surrender to some darker part of myself,
(for some nights, it is beyond my control)
my eyes flash open and I wonder,
why am I so willing?

perhaps we are all too blinded
by the appearance of perfection.
perhaps blindness strengthens our remaining senses.
how much time do we devote to being individuals,
and yet we are changed in one another's presence?
at what point do we become another person?
am I myself with him, or will I be with you?

will the trace of your fingertips along my wrist
push me to my bittersweet surrender,
or will it take more?
a conversation, a realization,
strong hands on my shoulders forcing me to cave.
you've caught me in your web.

haven't I always been afraid of spiders?
if you knew me, you might understand -
this longing for the kind of love
that makes promises rather than breaking them.
forever craving strength, loyalty,
(I found it)
but still I dream of you...

boston

hotter than the first of July,
and if everybody's got a hungry heart,
I'm about to swallow him with mine.

when you know

Teach me your methods — your calm and collected. My heart remains free while yours has arrested.

Tell me how to savour you. The flavour of you has me swallowing every drop with no intention to stop, sweet on my tongue as I choke and hum. Hand on your throat as your arms float overhead. Pinned to the bed but not yet mine. Give it time.

Give yourself over slowly. You'll never know lonely again. If and when you find yourself in this place I'm in — know you won't look back. A lack of control on my part, perhaps, but I lapse into reveries of an extension of the flawed perfection of our present tense.

Subtle hints of intentions as you mention distant plans and your hands send me skyward and your mouth grounds me once again. Matching my fire. My flames blaze higher with every kiss, and you are the slow and measured burn I've always missed.

Shelter me with your embrace at a modest pace. You are more than worth the wait. God or coincidence or fate brought you near. And here, when you know, you know.

Keep your heart under lock and key until you want little else but to open it to me.

a flood

portrait of a flight risk.
blood clocks in at 100 Celsius.
haven't the faintest clue what love is,
though I've felt its breath on my cheek.
hold me tonight and mind the fragility.
rake your fingers through my hair slowly.
listen to me talk about consciousness
and serial murder and dry-hopped beer.

kiss my forehead tenderly
when I've fallen asleep
halfway through a movie.
tell me your enduring fears,
deeply buried secrets,
and vividly painted memories
so that I might understand you
intimately... religiously.

accept my abundant flaws
and devote yourself to this lost cause.
cross the frayed rope bridge carefully,
for on the other side
lies everything I've spent my life
diligently half-concealing,
like the unconditional love
threatening to eviscerate me.

I may not know much of myself
with any certainty,
but I know that whomever
frees my heart from captivity
will be someone lucky.
for I have been holding back
a flood for nearly 26 years,
and someone ought to let it kill them.

I tried

I may have thought about you, but I tried not to.

It's less now, lesser than ever, though not entirely better. The new one took most of you away, but you're something of a clogged drain — not always obvious but certainly a bother when it counts. Long, slow, swirling, wasted moments spent watching you hang around.
Please, for the love of God, go down.

Perhaps if you didn't touch me accidentally. If the remnants of tension in quiet rooms didn't have me nearly biting through my bottom lip. If I didn't imagine you behind me gripping and tilting fluid hips. If I burnt the picture of you furious. The way a gentleman like you ought to be with me for whittling away at your resolve and turning it to agony. Door closed forcefully only to be pinned against it. Palm over my mouth, rhythm rattling hinges.

I have been practicing my platonic face. I think we are almost at the stage where we have erased any reminder of the desire I misplaced. Lost as always within your seaside gaze, feigning indifference but longing for an all-night taste.

I may have thought about you, but I tried not to.

all night

I slink outside
in a sundress,
find you on the porch
picking the strings
of a beat-up guitar,
boots tapping hardwood,
mouth set, immersed
in the music.

blissfully,
I sink into a chair,
bare ankles crossed,
palms perspiring,
clouds gathering in the sky,
humming along
as your voice
permeates the air.

your mischievous eyes
are fixed on me,
running all over me
like water
in the shower.
you bite your lip
between the verses,
never missing a beat.

I spring to my feet,
slip behind you,
fingertips light
on your neck
as you croon
a last note,
drop the guitar,
and grab me by the wrist.

we are nose to nose.
your irises are on fire.
my breath catches
in my throat
and the rain starts
its own song
on the tin roof.

the screen door
squeaks, slams
carelessly
behind us.
the air is cool
but we will be
warm all night.

blunt force trauma

I fixate and ruminate on what I cannot understand, and my heart is ever-present in your bloodstained hands.

I prefer not to make assumptions when I lack the opportunity for their confirmation, but my interpretation of your moonlit intention is to fill my thoracic cavity with aching apprehension.

Blunt force trauma from the sheer force of three words - and I wish you could have heard the audible gasp, the sharp rasp of my raspberry breath as I dizzily indulged in a lingering fantasy of your lips on my neck, pressed firmly to the seat back in a 2 a.m. taxicab, two travellers without a map or destination, lungs heavy with sweet anticipation, ventricles expelling scalding infatuation.

I think of the alleged impact — the crater's depth — and wonder if I truly crept beneath your skin or burned through what seemed a hostile atmosphere, and if I still appear, if only to sway and stumble about blind within the unlit alleyways of your restless mind.

A match not made in heaven but lit in hell. Between my claws and your venom, we knew just as well.

Ever intrigued by an air of mystery, yet your honesty leaves me tethered and craving either some reprieve or a truth I am forced, to one day believe.

the ghost

the vines of silence suffocate me,
daydreaming in sweet darkness.

there you were.
you were there.
were you there?

I wonder...

cold hands, hard liquor.
hearts bleeding with every beat.
living, yet slowly dying.

I'm writing love letters in my mind.
sugared kisses, sick passion.
trembling, starving.

hands tied
while you feed me lies.

there's no wind in my soul
to blow these ashes away.
I'll keep choking on your dust,
feeling your ghostly hands caress me,

as you lay beside her
imagining

what could have been.

melting

you're the candle
I can't resist
touching,
licking
my burnt lips
and fingertips,
cursing.

hypnotizing,
heat rising,
beguiling,
craving
more of
your warmth
on my skin.

melting
for you,
dripping,
dissolving,
igniting.
room aglow,
body ablaze.

raw

what am I to you?
an art exhibit?
an animal to rescue?
a fucking circus freak?

here you are again
outside my cage.

you draw near,
so I rattle the bars,
eyes bloodshot,
lips cracked.

(at least
you give me
permission
to show you
what I am.)

I paint murals
with colourful emotions,
scratch symphonies
into my skin,

choke on prophecies,
slow dance with demons,
run my tongue all over
these self-inflicted wounds.

what's it like out there?

you look like you drown yourself
in Novocaine
to avoid even the slightest trace
of pain.

what if I told you
it's not a flaw
to feel fiercely,
to be twisted
and tangled
and raw?

what if you
picked the lock,
held me in your arms,
felt the electricity in me,
our skin crawling?

would you
fear me?
revere me?

or would
you run?

tangled limbs and pounding hearts

to hear my name fall from your lips,
to be beside you when you wake.
the conversations we would have,
if all your time was mine to take.

in coffee shops and downtown cabs,
or on the porch beneath the stars.
on a boardwalk by the sea,
or tucked away in crowded bars.

raindrops falling on our skin
atop a craggy mountain's peak.
blanket spread on August grass,
sharing wine beside a creek.

Sunday mornings spent in bed,
tangled limbs and pounding hearts.
drunk and wild at 6 a.m.
before our southbound plane departs.

on sombre days when friends have passed,
when misery and pain prevail,
when bridges burn and bonds dissolve,
when all our dreams seem bound to fail...

I'll stand with you and face the storm.
I'll be your shelter when you break.
I'll love you for just what you are.
my soul was always yours to take.

secrets

a seed was planted
delicately.

untold truths
began to grow
like children
in her womb.

flourishing within,
developing magnificently
with each passing day.

she carried them lovingly,
though they stretched her skin,
pressed on her diaphragm
and nauseated her.

pregnant with
whispered secrets,
the day drew ever-near...

the day they'd spill forth,
tearing and torturing
as they made passage,
arriving in all their painful glory.

she would lay quietly,
exhaustedly admiring
the fragile creatures
that once shared her body.

(they are free now,
and they are screaming.)

waiting to break

what will come of me?
I am waiting to break, and it's only a matter of time
before this burden becomes too much for me to bear.
and where will it take me?
will I be hospitalized?
will I overmedicate with pills and drink?
will I think about slitting my wrists,
or swallowing a bottle of Clonazepam
and slumping beneath the bath water forever?
drowning would feel most familiar...
I have been sinking beneath the waves
of my own mind all the days of my life,
so it seems inevitable that I will grow tired
of waging wars,
and praying to gods who don't listen,
and listening to people who don't get it.
one of these days I will stop
swimming,
floating,
smiling,
lying,

and let it end me.

sinking

I see the artists
tumbling at your feet,
tripping on your wild words,
helplessly daydreaming of being
the reason for your
fervid musings.

but it was this
gypsy pyromaniac
who climbed aboard your ship,
and we set the damn thing on fire,
sinking hopelessly together,
our minds intertwined.

shooting heroin(e)

what were we,
if not a blazing catastrophe?
4 minutes, 12 seconds
replayed obsessively.
attempting to process,
digest all of this.
opening line plays,
imagining your
distended veins...
the look on your face,
before shooting me -
your heroin(e),
euphoria imminent,
taken in the car,
or anywhere really.
we were never very
reserved or tactful,
were we?
shrouded in darkness,
blindness amplifying
our other senses.
please... listen.
the vocabulary, rhymes
remind me of you.
metaphors multifaceted,

till in time they were
far more raw and blatant,
almost as if you were
under my influence.
and Jesus save us
... that rhythm -
a song made if only for dancing.
I know you would've,
while I stood there
grinning, embarrassed
and awkwardly swaying.
we were not forged
by slow dances... no.
we took off running
before we stole a car
and drove off at sunset
with the police chasing us.
but to be fair...
I'd rather not admit
that the thought of your body
pressed to mine
in a midnight kitchen
while moving ever-so-slowly
to the sound
of a record playing,

well, it haunts me.
you always asked me
what it was about me,
but I'm wondering
what it is about you.
on another note,
I wish the band knew
how much hope
and heartache was wrought
with one godforsaken song,
the catalyst for dramatic changes
in multiple relationships.
and the album title is ironic,
for modernity has indeed failed us,
and were our relationships
conducted only offline, I imagine
it wouldn't have played out like this,
with me driving recklessly
and restarting it over and over again.
I am dichotomous.
perhaps that's what it is.
and in stark contrast
to my vicious independence,
I have this aching, gaping,
palpable emptiness reserved
for a love never given

the way I can give it,
when the switch is on and fixed,
longing to have it, if it even exists.
drown you in affection
but somehow always keep you guessing,
call you daddy and mother your children,
and fight about whether
they'd have blue or brown eyes.
the thought of it was nice.
but truth is only hearsay,
and I'm not sure
I'm as addictive as you say.

love charade

We drink cheap whiskey and smoke haphazardly out the window screen till the roofs of our mouths are raw. And we play indie records like hipsters and we love to argue about who's more like Bukowski and we scream-read our poetry till the next-door neighbours are slamming on the wall saying 'shut the fuck up.' But we mishear them, so we shut up and fuck, and your hand clasps my mouth to stifle the moans, and your drunk eyes are cold but your body warms and fills and floods me. And perfection is a myth but when we play this love charade, I feel strangely content.

expectations

a sea of glittering bodies
twisting and grinding,
humming and writhing,
drumbeat reverberating,
ballroom approaching
its collective climax.
but I am unfortunately
not similarly stimulated —
clipped smile simulated,
perched on a barstool
like a sad little harlot,
coating the edges
of a champagne glass
with violet lipstick,
gazing at the barman
and his very thick
tattooed neck
till he notices, grins,
thinks I'm into him,
refills my glass.
and I am all alcohol
and little white pills,
pearls and stiletto heels,
bitching to anyone
who'll listen about
not having a man,

and boy, do men
love to fucking listen.
carefully calculating,
looking for a way in,
and the weed I vaped
before I came in
has me higher than
my expectations of men.
the sky is falling,
the ball is dropping,
and I'll cut you
if you try to kiss me.

broken-heart syndrome

my heart is anatomically large,
a quivering lump in my mediastinum.
its affliction has a dismal cause -
they call it broken-heart syndrome.

edematous, ineffective walls,
atypical left ventricular contraction.
this peculiar lapse in systolic function,
triggered by his fading attraction.

teeth clenched as knifelike pain
carves through muscle with a serrated blade.
tachypneic from the constant ache,
in pooling thoughts of death, I wade.

with a stethoscope of ice you'll hear
the parting words of a murmuring heart.
the arrhythmic beats intensify:
a shrill scream, 'get the crash cart!'

this butchered, swollen mass has failed.
no push of adrenaline will suffice.
try as you may to defibrillate me,
this mottled corpse will not die twice.

cause of death: cardiac arrest
due to takotsubo cardiomyopathy.
losing him is what did me in -
don't bother yourself with an autopsy.

drunk on you

if you see me on the street
under white twinkling lights,
bundled in a toque and mittens,
cheeks flushed poinsettia red
in your presence,
snowflakes sparkling
as they melt on thick lashes,
black eyes pooling with
dishonourable intentions...
I hope you quell the storm in me
with a whispered plea.

two sets of footprints
leading to your cabin,
fireplace crackling,
top-shelf rum
and eggnog to drink,
Elvis on the record machine
singing Blue Christmas
as you wrap me in your arms
like a present.

throw me down beneath the tree,
tinsel and evergreen falling
all around us.

sugarplum kisses
on candy cane lips,
flannel shirts on the floor
and a blizzard outside,
making love
like it's December 25th,
too drunk on you to care
when Christmas is.

reversed polarity

My navigational abilities are to be desired. An internal compass rife with malfunction. Iron lungs eliciting magnetic deviation. My selection of direction conducted on a whim without a care for where the moonlit path may lead. And knowing better than to meddle or fix, you accounted for my reversed polarity without an attempt to recalibrate my ornate imbalance.

Drawn to your magnetism, I imagined a reality with a set destination. But beholding the blazing beacon on my own intuition, I was wary of proceeding to where you might be leading. And thus I spun in the opposite direction with haste to retrace my own meandering footprints. Hoping to erase the ache of your absence as it gnawed at my flesh, tearing to the depths of my heaving chest. Unable to give you the time of day when you asked as I myself did not know it. In my bones I felt the darkness had only begun, that the night was young and unending perils were destined to come.

And you watched me run with the knowledge that all along we were only minutes from dawn. Dazzling light caressing every cavern and crevice, casting away looming shadows and crippling misconceptions.

And as the rising sun lit my westward path I gasped, glancing back to the east, tangerine horizon framing a glass-like sea. An apologetic silhouette that never chased as I left, not lacking in desire but abounding in respect. My consciousness this time accepting a heartfelt proclamation as you bled and I fled, this time in your direction. Reuniting in a graveyard to bury our transgressions.

377 miles of separation as I imagine your arms tight around me, refusing to let me slip away in the dead of night or light of day. Your face buried in my hair, as I press my ear near your heart if only to comprehend the ferocity with which it beats for me.

Ask me as you have to stay so that I may, fingers interlaced as we stand quietly in the fading light, abandoning lingering narratives of loneliness as darkness approaches and we embrace beneath it.

love, or the idea of it

I am a healer only because
I need healing myself.
I don't do well in seeking help.
I never had that luxury.
I self-medicate with enough
cigarettes and alcohol
and antidepressants
to render the loneliness acceptable.

on rare occasions when I meet someone
who seems to understand my mind,
I am pulled toward them gravitationally
and their effect is unmatched —
for there is nothing more intimate
than to be understood and still, accepted.

love, to others has two forms —
the heart-wrenching ailment that is
new love, and better still,
the easy acceptance of flaws,
the bickering and coexisting happily.

for me, there is a third form
that transcends appearances
and lust
and general reason.

a love of the soul.
a love that disregards
the usual parameters,
and so is generally
doomed or forbidden.

this love
(or the idea of it)
consumes me,
fills my fragile head
with words, so many words,
with songs and paintings
and half-remembered dreams.

I destroy myself over it
(or the idea of it.)
I spread myself carelessly
on the railroad,
teeth clenched, back arched,
waiting for the freight train
to obliterate me.

drifting

I was green once,
flourishing, undefiled,
feigning immortality
for as long as summer held me.

you crept upon me then,
skeletal autumn hands
shrouding me in frost,
colouring me crimson.

how transient a vibrance,
how cataclysmic a dissolution.
our hearts like leaves drifting,
exposing barren branches.

blue velvet

I like it when you tell me
what to do.

unzip your lips
and your dress, too.

velvet fabric falling,
wrapped in strong arms, wanting.

lips parting,
skin on skin, starving.

kill me
softly.

Cardinal

this town feels haunted.

the bar down the street opens
on Thursdays and Saturdays,
but nobody's there.

an old shirtless man stares
when I drive by.
I wave,
but he doesn't return it.
just keeps on staring
with those dead, beady eyes.

the church bells ring for hours
like a broken music box
that won't shut up
unless you smash it
over and over
on the dresser.

seems the only time
the town gets busy
is for a funeral.

cars line the streets,
strange, solemn people
shuffle around
apologetically.

the air smells grainy.
spiders collect, crawl
up the siding
on the walls
of our houses,
lazily building webs
as we sleep upstairs
with the windows open.

you can hear
the early morning drawl
of the ships' horns
as they pass in the fog,
angry waves beating
against the shore;
already weary
from the thaw.

the kids are pale.
they put their hoods up
in the rain,
waiting for the bus,
waiting for time to pass,
waiting to get a licence
to drive away,
never come back.

the stars are bright.
the wind is crisp.
and it's quiet...
eerily quiet.
except for
those damn
church bells.

dose increase

the beast numbed by white pills
claws from deep within,
whispering its sinister reminder —
I am still fighting.
reluctant breath comes in rasps.
that old familiar ache
penetrates bleak, grey organs
tucked beneath gaunt ribs.
these ducts are too medicated
to produce tears.
quietly despairing, anticipating
the inevitable shattering
of composure,
the illness' return.
a withdrawal from all
or a frantic fall into toxic arms.
loss of purpose, hopelessness,
crippling fear of loneliness.
dark rooms and wasted days,
unpaid sick leave,
dysphoric mood, crippling anxiety.
I'm so tired of feeling everything.
guess I'll try 30mg instead of 20.

sex and cigarettes

we're wasting time,
both unwilling
to swallow our pride.
eaten alive in the night
by rogue dreams
of sailboats and sand,
stars and hotel beds,
sex and cigarettes.

these tension-laced looks
will be the death of me.
my heart can't take
the way you make it race,
the way you possess me.
I need a fix for this addiction.
I need to have you
in my system.

lonely in love

The sun is setting and my mouth tastes like stale cigarettes, so I take a sip of lukewarm tea to kill it, readjusting the blanket around my shoulders and shivering as I stand beside the cold, empty woodstove, gazing out the window.

You're out there with an axe in your hand in a t-shirt that might have once been white, and it's sticking to your chest. Even from here I can see the beads of sweat on your brow, the sawdust in the air settling on the scruff on your clenched jaw as you swing the blade through the air and it comes down mercilessly on the wood. And I think later you will be the axe, and I, the slab of pine, and you'll be harsh with me, and I will shatter and split underneath you.

With a sixth sense keenly refined to feel my eyes, you perceive me as I shamelessly watch you run a hand through ebony hair. You take a long look behind you into the woods, gazing up at the tops of the trees before glancing knowingly through the glass at me, lips spreading into a smile that blinds me, or maybe it's the light in the sky behind you, but I blink a few times trying to figure it all out and come up with nothing other than that there is a higher power up there somewhere and they are on my side.

I tiptoe in bare feet to the squeaky screen door and out onto the frigid patio stones, the fall wind biting my ankles, dark leaves tossed around grimly in the air. You meet me there with an armful of firewood, the veins in your forearms distended, smile still blinding, and your free hand rests for just a moment on my hip as you pass by me.

We build a roaring fire together and move the chairs next to it and sip whiskey and talk about buying this place and staying out here in the woods in the quiet with the windows open at night, listening to the wolves and the wind howl, and I think about what a life that would be — you and I locked up in a cabin, all lonely in love.

friction

friction

between us as we fight,
rub each other the wrong way,
looks and bodies laced with tension.

friction

your hand, my wrist.
cursing you as you lift my face
to yours and I so readily submit.

friction

your sandpaper scruff
buried in that delicate place,
writhing, back arching to meet you.

friction

skin raw and reddened,
knuckles white half the night,
relentlessly pursuing shared ecstasy.

you, me

rain on a tin roof,
warm blanket,
dark room,
you,
me,
long kisses,
steady hands,
all I'll ever need.

unapologetic

it's always been me —
myself alone.
the only one
worth counting on.
and I feel sometimes
the pang of longing,
but I don't need
you or anyone.
I don't need to be
held or saved.
and when you see
me reaching out,
you assume
I'm insecure
or narcissistic,
but it's connection
I'm seeking,
not validation.
it's always been me,
talking myself down.
six years old
on the playground,
ten and depressed,
unnoticed.
thirteen, sobbing,
knife to my wrist.

sixteen, giving away
my virginity carelessly
to get it over with.
nineteen and naïve,
abused emotionally,
too anxious
to eat or sleep,
binge drinking,
knife to my wrist.
twenty-three,
drugged and raped,
feigning composure,
internally tortured.
twenty-five
and turbulent,
still unsure
what it is I crave.
running away from
the commitment
I thought I wanted,
starting over,
rebuilding,
resilient,
alone again
and unapologetic.

and if you want to be
part of this life
I've made,
know that I will
carry on whether
you choose
to leave or stay.

it's always been me.

grappling

I like to think
most afternoons
you're slumped
in a parked car
thinking of me,

glitching out,
closing those
heavy eyelids,
submitting to an
unconscious fix.

imagining this
plaid shirt hanging
off my shoulders
just before it drops
in slow motion.

the curve of my spine
under candlelight,
sugar-laced lips,
your hands tight
around my hips.

I like to think
of you grappling
with better judgement,
trying to resist
how tempting this is.

derailed

I'm a train wreck, yes —
a smoldering catastrophe.
but let's not forget
who fucking derailed me.

don't stop

I am not what you know.
this skin, like ice
beneath your sandpaper palms,
these lips, desperate
and warm against yours.
this thin, fading frame,
so easy to manipulate,
to carry to bed
or throw against the door.
dark, tortured eyes
wide and locked to yours,
a smirk on your lips
that makes my heart skip...
this is it.
inexplicable connection.
hearing you gasp,
our frantic need met.
two bodies becoming one
in rhythmic escalation.
so forceful at first
that I curse at you
when your pace slows.
and you push these wrists
deep into the mattress,
carrying on the agony,

watching my body
arch and bend to yours.
basking in the look
of desperation I give
before you oblige
my strangled pleas
with ferocity.
these fingernails nearly
slicing through your back.
not so much lovemaking
as a ruthless attack.
your weight and warmth
enveloping me,
your face buried in my neck
as you fill me so adeptly.
your breath quickening
as you lift your head
and meet my hungry eyes
just before
our climactic collapse,
trembling together,
covered in sweat.
I am not what you know,
but don't stop
until you've memorized
every inch of me.

rocket fuel

overtaken by words,
assaulted by fantasies.
you — the rocket fuel,
and I — the vessel,
launched into oblivion,
alone among the stars,
tangled in the throes
of ill-placed desire.
every sense amplified,
hearing colours, tasting music,
madness rattling
around in my skull.
flames licking bridges,
mountains crumbling
as I spin gleefully,
feet seared by hot coals.
summoning the lightning,
daring the skies
to have their way with me.
to be that fearless,
to crash catastrophically,
to be beaten and bruised
by my own careless fiction...

the affliction nearing death,
I watched it set
on an oceanfront horizon,
clung to it desperately,
pressed it to my chest,
but my severed arteries
had already bled out
every crimson drop of poetry.

I don't want to be sane again
if it means putting down my pen.

strange

how strange a species we are,
pretending life has such value
and doing everything in our power
to kill ourselves a little quicker.

circling the drain

evolving again,
don't know what I am.
used to be painted,
now, I watch
the pretty colours
circling the drain,
staining the bathtub
magenta and turquoise,
and I am just grey.
I either need
to learn to breathe,
or better still,
drink myself to sleep.
I want to be to you
what you are to me.
I need to tie myself
to something — anything,
so that this time
I don't run.
I always fucking run.
predictable in
my instability,
I'm not even good
at being bad now.

can't begin to dream
of anything permanent
when life isn't.
over here wishing
for things I don't have.
what an existence...
everybody's sad,
or is it just me?
do you get like this?
are you going to call me
and tell me I'm depressed?
put me under
water or sedation.
it hurts too much
coming down
from these highs.
throw me in the trenches
or send me to the sky.
mourn me while I live,
smile when I die.

a burning question

did you smoke a cigarette
after you mind-fucked me?

reckless

give her obsession,
unhealthy fixation.
let her see
the torment pooling
in your ice-blue eyes,
cursing and revering
the way she dances
out of your grasp
when you try
to pull her close.

stay awake all night
thinking of
her fevered lips on yours,
the way her mind works,
mixed messages,
electric glances,
slim chances.
her hips, and her hair,
and her reckless disregard
for your sanity.

too

I'm shut off or cranked, but there's no in between. No medium heat. I don't simmer. I'm one of two things — glacier or incinerator. You'll find me indifferent, or crazed and obsessive. And when it comes to you, I'm the latter. I can't say I had much say in the matter.

Something about your presence (and admittedly, your absence) draws out the parts of me I wanted to believe I had exterminated. The utter insanity. The cravings. The suffocating and aching. Face pressed to your pillow just to breathe in the scent you left behind. Wishing I could have you all the time as you place yourself intentionally at a distance. There's not enough medication or smoke or beer in the world to lull me into indifference.

I try to make you an addiction, knowing you long for a calm progression. You want reality, not heaven. My demeanor may indicate that capability but let me assure you of my utter instability... my compulsion to place my beating heart in your hands before you've even committed to this weekend's plans.

I wish I could meet someone who appeals to me and not find myself imagining a log cabin tucked away in the woods, forearms encircling my waist on a lazy Sunday as

I make pancakes or the sound of children running barefoot down the hall. It isn't you who does this to me — it's me. And yet you tear it and my guts right out of me.

You should have known when you pulled me against you in that king bed and planted your lips on my forehead that I would be smitten. That looking at me with fiery irises would trigger my romanticism.

Would you prefer too much or not enough? Fierce loyalty or fabricated love? Merciless pleasure or a slap on the hand? Breathtaking intensity or something bland?

Too clingy. Too emotional. Too idealistic. Too anxious. Too overwhelming. Too deep. Too messed up tonight to sleep. Too fucking into you. But tell me... what else is new?

loving me is a death sentence

lately,
my poetry hovers
between wanting you
and wanting to wreck
every man in existence.

this cigarette-burnt heart
longs to end it all,
to overdose on beer
and benzodiazepines
or throw itself off a cliff.

and it beats
a little less violently when
it does not have a muse to ruminate upon.
and its rhythm is fragmented
when it thinks of you.

and it does not have a rewind button.
and its hard drive cannot be wiped.
and these memories do not become
less vivid with the passage of time.
and it aches.

and time does not heal all wounds.
and loving me is a death sentence.

and there are always conditions.
and this pounding mass in my chest
is bloodthirsty.

and it is wrapped in electric fence.
and everyone who dares reach for me
ends up frothing at the mouth
and convulsing.
so tell me,

how do I open it?

the muse

cover my mouth with tape
and tie my hands behind me,
so they cannot reach
for paper and ink,
so that my tongue
does not reveal
my vulnerability.
hush my lips —
your turn to speak.
tell me I haunt you.
that the thought of me
consumes you.
tell me my touch ignites
every wanting inch of you.
so many moons
I've been aching for you -
tonight, let me be the muse.

lightning

your voice —
gentle,
commanding,
reminiscent
of lazy days
in mid-July.
dark room,
darker skies,
listening to
the lawless
melody
of rain
on the
tin roof.

heavy clouds
overhead,
summer storm
fast-approaching,
thunder
rattling
the windowpane.
trembling
underneath you,
bracing,

anticipating
your lips
and the lightning
electrocuting.

human

she paints her nails candy pink
and reads Bukowski,
dreaming of a world
where her words make her money.

she could lay in her bed
all week, drunk,
wearing rose lingerie
and conjuring up the sort of men
who could handle her.

they live in the poems
with their dark, messy hair,
heartbreak eyes,
and chiseled bodies
that would overpower
her waning frame.

it's hard to eat
when you hate the way
things are,
and things are only
getting worse,
and you are getting older
with every breath.

and your heart permanently races
from the caffeine you tell yourself
you need just to stay alive,
but we are all dying anyway.

the test never ends,
and we never find out
the answers,
let alone if we passed
or if
we killed ourselves
trying.

cigars and stiff drinks

things that are
bad for me
taste too good —
cigars,
stiff drinks,
and you.

carry on

you say you'll love me till the end
as you build yourself a fallout shelter.

you won't come out to dance
in the acid rain, but I understand.

all this time you've tried
so desperately not to feel pain.

you avoid anything explosive,
so naturally, you fear

the temperature of my skin,
the hot blood in my veins.

you could learn to love the pain,
walk with me through the flames,

surrender,
feel it all,

or carry on
half alive.

the end

am I transparent to you?

can you see
right through me,
when you pick me up
like a book
and read me?

do you sigh when
you breathe in
the familiar scent
of perfume and paper,
when you peruse
these tattered pages?

do I feel good
on your tongue
when you read
these words aloud?
is it refreshing to wade
in the depths of me?

do I appear there
on the edge of the bed?

when you think of me,
can you almost feel
the heat of my breath,
my mouth on your neck?

will you delve into
the darker chapters,
get acquainted with
my twisted desires,
drink whiskey
with my demons?

will it all
be too much?
will you slam
the cover shut,
tuck me away
for another day?

or will you cling to me?
will I be
the one thing
you've found
you can't seem
to put down?

after the climax,
will you stay
and tear out
the last page?
will you rewrite
the end of my story?

between the lines

it's back again.

it sinks into me the way
I sink beneath the water in the bath.
it likes to stay afloat
while I hold my breath
under the surface
thinking of
death.

all the bubbles will be gone
by the time they find me.

how did I get like this?

de·pressed
/də ' prest
(of a person) in a state of general unhappiness or
despondency.

words aren't enough.

sitting, so serene,
a moment later,
shaking, desperate.

trying to drown it
with love and sex,
still doesn't work,
smoke cigarettes.

fantasies of
12-packs and
bottles full of pills.

tell who you want,
but they won't know how to

(help.)

bones

I long to crawl
between
your neurons
and watch the way
the chemicals
dance at your
synapses.

breathe me in
like air,
so that I might
fill your lungs
and oxygenate
your blood
and live inside you
for a moment,
until I escape
your lips
like a sigh.

I dream I am
one of the fibres
that hold your
heart in place;

that I am
trembling
and present
in every
delicious
dichotomous beat.

I know you feel
my fingers on your wrists,
my legs on your shoulders,
my lashes on your cheek.

but say you feel me
like I feel you,

in my bones.

days like this

the tide moves me,
and it's like
loving someone
for the first time.
I always dreamed
it would feel this way.
bright and new,
shiver after shiver
caressing my spine.
tangled hair,
ocean air,
sweet music
of crashing waves.
chilling water,
bare legs.
standing here,
sun falling
for a distant horizon,
and I get wondering
about the meaning of it all —
and I think
this is it.
we are here,
we are alive,
if only for days
like this.

hardwired to hurt

there is
certainly
no honour
in feeling
everything
as we do —
intensely.

those of us
hardwired
to hurt
frantically
search for
something
to numb it,

or we write
in tear-stained
notebooks
deliriously
about people
who will never
understand us.

the bridge

under the bridge,
the river runs fiercely,
its current unrelenting.

a transport truck
bound for New York
rattles steel rails eerily.

beneath, the cargo ships
drift past rugged men
in small fishing boats —

they who brave wind,
whitecaps and rain
for a modest catch.

come night, the silence
deafens, the trek long
as air chills restless bones.

climbing over rails,
hovering precariously
over the mirror-like water below.

closed eyes fantasize
of skin colliding fatally
against the frigid moonlit surface.

found in a few days,
floating face-down,
gazing tragically into the depths.

but again,
I talk myself off that ledge —
another day not dead.

prison

you couldn't fathom
the images
these broken neurons
fashion from
the thinnest threads
of unease.

you couldn't dream
of what I swallow,
suppress,
slather in blood
on the walls of this
flesh-covered prison.

ce soir

I did my nails pale pink,
bought some houseplants,
(jasmine and pilea)
drove around aimlessly,
fell asleep on the couch,
put on dark lipstick,
played the piano,
watched ships on the river,
went to French class,
(il va pleuvoir ce soir)
crawled in bed,
tried to write,
but tonight,
there are no words —
only a dull ache
and a blissful dream
of you.

life sentence

blue lights flash,
reflecting in bloodshot sclera,
and I'd love to be chased on his interstate.
in this particular case, I wouldn't disappear
without a trace of DNA remaining.
he could memorize my fingerprints
and hold me for days.
I'd succumb to his arresting gaze,
pleading guilty and doing time
for every whispered crime,
stealing kisses from my jailor
behind the bars of a welcome cage,
serving a life sentence without parole
or any desire to escape.

capsized

I rolled in
with the tide
to a seaside bar,
found you there
hiding beneath
the brim of your hat,
gazing into your glass.
I laid a gentle hand
on your taut, brown arm
and found myself capsized
by your eyes,
bluer than the bay,
as you offered me
the other rickety chair.
and we shared
margaritas and wild stories,
hearts thudding to the beat
of the reggae that was playing.
drawn away hours later
by the afternoon heat,
we ran for the shore,
tossing clothes along the way.
wet lips and sunburnt skin,
white sand and bare feet,
wading in so deep.

dancing our way
along the beach
to your place,
hotter still
all tangled up
in bedsheets,
drifting off
to the sound
of easy breath
and crashing waves.
waking at sunrise
to your island eyes
all over me,
tasting salt
on your lips
as you whispered
'stay.'

pieces

I've been looking for you in the raspberry patches.

The fruit is hardly ripe, but there's a handful there. A taste. I spend my hours searching under the midday sun only to trudge home with an empty bucket and a heavy heart, my bare legs scratched and bleeding. I hardly feel the thorns when they tear at my flesh. Some might call me passionate; others would say I'm obsessed.

Really darling, what does it matter? I'm tired of catering to everyone's perceptions. If there's a glitch in your brain, only you can consciously commit to building a new circuit. If you think that emotion is a flaw, you ought to find yourself a nice lady without a soul and the two of you will get along just fine.

Gone are the days where I'll apologize for the corners of my mouth tightening, for hot tears streaming down my freckled cheeks. If you're in the passenger's seat and we're driving down a summer road, chances are I'll sing like you're not even there.

I traded reckless tendencies for awareness. I live in an upscale A-frame with a rust-coloured roof and meticulously planted gardens. The air is hot in my upstairs bedroom, but when I open the patio doors the breeze blows in and the white blinds dance to and fro.

At night I can hear the distant highway traffic, transport brakes on the bridge, the mumble of the television downstairs, the hum of my grandparents chatting on the front porch, the splatter of rain on the tin roof above.

I've got a pack of menthols in the car that I haven't touched in weeks. I haven't touched a man in weeks either. I ought to be more meticulous. The next notch in my belt is a double digit.

I look back on it all and realize I haven't been made love to — at least not in the way it plays out in daydreams. There's always a hiccup — a lack of love or a sense of fear or a certain incompatibility. I've carelessly consented to being stretched and contorted, to a brief sense of fullness that leads to lasting emptiness. Sometimes I get nauseous thinking about the things I've done.

This sweet solitude seems to be slowly filling the fissures of my soul. I spend my days working and cooking and running on empty roads at sunset. My skin is dark now, and it has a different kind of glow. I think I'm almost ready.

All my dreams will realign when I have you at last. When I no longer need wealth or recognition to distract me from your absence.

I could run a laboratory or we could open a brewery. I could be a healer or a mother or I could paint the river from this second-story balcony and show my art every Sunday at the farmer's market. I could sell a million copies of our love story.

We could live here, or somewhere where all the seasons feel like summer. I could wake in the dead of night and watch the threads of moonlight dancing on your face. I could brush your soft lips with my fingertip and watch you stir, grimace a little and pull me against you. Your breath will be warm on my skin.

And you won't leave an inch of skin untouched. My heart will be free and our tea will be warm and our eyes will lock together when we make love. We'll hide away for days every chance we get.

Wherever you are, I hope you're smiling. When you find me, I know — all of our pieces will make the perfect whole.

falling

the bricks I've laid
around my heart
to keep you out
are poorly placed.

you come around,
I crumble.

a spring that never comes

our love was once
scorching summer,
sunburnt shoulders
and drunken kisses,
starlight dripping
from the oblivion,
raw skin glistening,
blissfully ignorant
of our gradual
transformation.

fall, vividly painted
a thousand colours,
emotions heightened,
bursting forth
from heavy branches,
free-falling down
toward harsh ground,
teeth clenched,
clinging to a climax
we couldn't sustain.

we are frigid now.

the air that stings
our fragile lungs
escapes chapped lips
in bitter exhales.
we shiver as if it were
the dead of winter,
rubbing sticks together,
trying to relight
a dying fire,
wondering if spring
will ever find us.

LINGERIE

these thoughts
are lingerie,
whirling around
in the machine
that is my mind.
my pen is a clothespin;
I hang myself out to dry.

you think I should keep
the delicates inside,
but they feel better
on my skin when
they are blown around
all day in the wind,
and everyone can see them
as they're walking by.

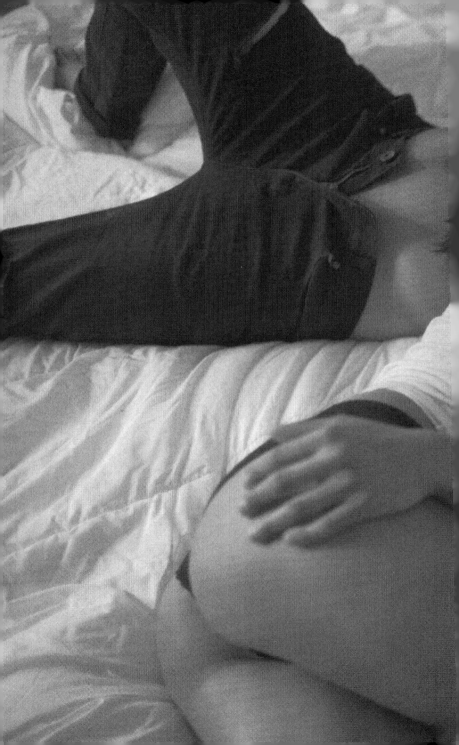

WHO YOU COULD HAVE BEEN

I loved you when you were a wish —
when I dreamt of having you,
not knowing that I would.
when science and reason said
you were insignificant,
I imagined all you might become,
felt your gentle spirit thriving,
felt my body morphing into a haven for you.
felt weak while wanting to give you
everything on earth,
wondered if your eyes would be dark brown,
if you'd have his smile,
or if I could love you right —
make you feel like you were magic,
like you had a place in this world.
but as it happened, you didn't.
and now I have only a million different ideas
of who you could have been,
and an emptiness I can't seem to shake.

in it

Should I listen to the warnings you give me between the moments you indulge me, or should I carry on like this, blindly believing that you could be everything I've found myself imagining?

I am likely not as delusional as you and those who read me think. There is much for us to someday face beyond sleepless nights and lazy mornings, midnight musings and freeway speeding. My love cannot fix everything. And my intention is not to repair, but rather to be there in spite of everything. To be a constant in the moments you doubt permanence. And the consistency of my presence is remarkable considering the cynicism that tends to cloud my perception. You shone through my darkness with your affection. Yet here I am again with a reason to prioritize my own protection. Should I?

Tell me what it is I ought to do. Tell me I can trust myself with you. Tell me the parts of you that want to love freely will outweigh your destructive tendencies.

I am many things but I am not everything. There will always be qualities you admire that I do not possess, interests you have that will never consume me. Parts of me I will not give away carelessly. Facets of my being that are less than appealing. But I have long since given up my own careless daydream of perfection. It never exists, and love requires commitment through the bitter and ugly. I know this despite my history of running.

And perhaps it's ridiculous that I'm musing over this already, but I am not one to fuck around with trivial things. I am not one to collect hearts and names. I know what I seek and I know that you speak to parts of me no man ever has. Fault me on that, if you wish.
Condemn me for my openness. I value honesty above all else and you have adjusted to my desire for it, despite its inevitable effects. Yet as much as honesty, I crave loyalty. An effort to let me be the centre of everything. Selfish, perhaps, but I am what I am. Forgive me for wanting you to myself. Forgive me for not wanting to imagine you with someone else in any sense.

You cannot possess me wholly if I am not enough entirely. I see the way you want me to be. I see the ways you've opened yourself to me against all odds, and somehow despite the turmoil we've put each other through, you've found your way back to me and I to you.

Thoughts and conversations rational despite the intensity of our emotions, attempting to build a foundation for something greater than this. I know what it is.

And despite the walls you've long-since collapsed somewhere deep within this aching chest, despite the manner in which they now attempt to reassemble themselves — you tell me you're in it, and I hardly question it before reminding you how deeply I have found myself in it too.

attraction to distraction

pay the bills,
take the pills.

less crazy,
more hazy.

keep working
harder... harder!

you've got
an attraction
to distraction.

'cause when you spend
any length of time
alone with your mind,
things tend to get ugly.

when you read me

I want you here
across this battered table,
squinting at the setting sun,
lighting a cigarette,
drawing it in
indulgently,
silver smoke
escaping parted lips
as you hand it over,
your fingertips
hesitating
against mine.

I need only
your presence,
your willingness
to hear me confess
my wild sins,
till the town sleeps
and the only light upon us
comes from
the glowing moon,
the porch light flickering,
talking till morning,
drowning in dreams,
divulging all our darkness.

you have a way
about you —
a calmness,
a depth.
and I know
when you read me,
when you run
your trembling hands
over these pages,
something
feels familiar.

drowning in Portland

pack your things.
tell them anything
but the truth,
and I'll meet you at 8.
we can drive all day
till we hit the coast of Maine,
the late afternoon sun
warming our shoulders
as we stroll by the sea
in Portland,
the gulls circling round
the lobster shacks,
looking for a morsel.

sit next to me by the docks
on a weathered bench.
brush the hair from my face
for a moment,
till the wind has its way
and messes it again.
sunlight all around me,
right hand on your thigh,
lighthouses reflecting
in your eyes.

tossing back oysters
on a patio at dusk,
laughing as we swig
strong beer,
the bitterness making
our tongues tingle
as we reminisce,
daydream about
hours and years to come,
never once mentioning
how good 'now' feels.

dancing in the moonlight
to slow, sultry jazz,
piano keys and hearts
pounding, swaying,
fingers interlocked,
hovering precariously
on the edge of this
becoming more
than a one-shot getaway.

midnight beach sand
slipping between
our fingertips,

daring you to
follow me
into unfamiliar waters,
memorizing the sight
of you plunging
beneath the surface,
rising only to
pull me down too.
drowning in
this ocean,
this moment
and you.

the best part

you tell me my scars
are the best part of me
as you trace my neck
with a cool blade —
a slow, sensual threat
to slice me wide open.

careful

you go on about
wanting a woman
who tells it like it is,

then you find her,
and you wish
she would stop
with her
damn honesty
and just tell you
what you want
to hear.

(careful what
you wish for.)

volcanic

I find myself
tracing his initials
on the corners of the pages
where I've scrawled sweet love stories
that will never come to fruition.

I dream up candied melodies
and can nearly feel
his mouth on my ear,
singing those lyrics acapella —
my lips, my shoulders, his fingertips.

there's a trend;
it seems I chase the unattainable,
do the unthinkable,
and somehow, I am forgiven for causing hurricanes
because I destroy myself too.

my heart is hardwired to fear the semblance of love,
unconvinced that anyone
could ever feel the forest fire
igniting my magma blood,
my volcanic soul.

and darling, my craving for you
when I've yet to possess you
is electrifying.
a primal ache, an itch, an insatiable thirst
to have you and to hold you and to hurt you.

'fix it,' he says,
as if rewiring the brain is a simple feat,
as if one day sex turns into love,
and the paralyzing fear
of commitment magically subsides.

there must be a forgotten stanza
where I drown
in the ocean of a man's existence,
where I learn to be happy in one version of forever,
where I stop imagining something more.

weak without a vice

along with the mystery,
the words have left me.
I am a fruitless tree,
barren and bleak,
another muse dissolving
before my weary eyes.

I try to write
about a rodeo cowboy I met,
about an abusive ex,
but the lines
don't flood the paper right.

and it isn't the same
without my neurons
screaming your name,
without your toxic current
coursing through me.

I ought to be at peace,
but to the contrary
I am weak without a vice —
desire has always been
the best kind of high.

but I settled today
for weed and mimosas,
for little white pills
and a pack of Pall Malls.
my throat is closing up,
but I swear I'm okay.

space

you are the earth
beneath my feet,

and all I want
is space.

hard to break

you swept in with the clouds
and I saw nothing
but lightning flashing in your eyes,
felt nothing but your storm.

I strayed off course,
wind tearing at my sails
as you summoned the rain
and kept my eye from shore.

I tried in vain to hold the wheel,
but chaos reigned;
spinning the ship, my heart,
in sickening circles.

lost at sea, I lost me —
forgot who I had been.
you came so close
to lifting the anchor from the sand.

just when I feared
it wouldn't end,
the rain fell softly
and the fog began to lift.

I stood there,
drenched and weary,
shivering
on the deck.

your thunder echoes
further still away,
the ocean waves and I
easing as you fade.

you were tireless,
dangerous,
and when you moved me
you were strong.

but unlike you,
I'm hard to break —
you only had me
for so long.

in October

His eyelids flutter just before dawn, and he surfaces from the depths of a haunting dream, stretching groggy limbs. The room is pitch dark and cold, the silence deafening as he slips from beneath the patchwork quilt, his bare feet recoiling at the first feel of the frigid floor. Shrugging on a flannel shirt and donning thick socks and well-worn jeans, an early morning smile spreads across his face.

He yawns and makes the trek down stairs that ominously creak, blindly feeling his way to the kitchen where he flicks the light and the coffee pot on. Despite the hour, this is his favourite time of day — the time before the rest of the world tends to wake.

The fireplace is still lukewarm from the evening before, the buried coals ignite the newspaper and finely split kindling wood he assembles atop them, and before long, firewood crackles away.

Steaming coffee in hand, he slides open the patio door with a blanket draped over his broad shoulders. The air is as crisp as one expects in October, the sun creeping hesitantly over the horizon. He breathes in deeply, melts into an Adirondack chair and closes his eyes indulgently,
basking in the autumn silence.

The day is young and he finds his solace here on a rickety veranda in the middle of nowhere, not a soul around for miles, save for the wild animals.

The solitude soothes his grieving soul. He is still as the leaves fall around on the ground in shades of vibrant orange, pastel yellow, blood red and rust brown. The trees rustle eerily in the breeze. Soon their branches will be barren again and the frost will harden the ground, and in the mornings the floorboards will be colder still, the firewood piled higher, and he will need a heavy coat out here.

And in the daytime he will be alright, but he will feel her ghostly hands at night, her cold feet pressed against his legs. He'll wake at 1 a.m. to the gentle sound of her breath and turn on the light frantically only to find himself alone in that bed yet again, still not quite believing that she's dead.

games

these words
I write
resonate,

hemorrhaging
from synapses,
bleeding onto paper.

you tell me
how they
make you feel,

and we both pretend
they aren't about you.

6:48

She slumps forward onto a weathered table. It's fucking noisy out — the speaker next to her blasting 'Can't You See', a multitude of birds in a nearby tree chirping maniacally, church bells loud as shit (and they won't stop for at least half an hour), motorcycles rumbling by on the Highway 2, random pie plate in the neighbour's yard smacking around, wind jostling the papers in the recycling bin.

The sun is glorious, bringing the bronze tone back to her arms. Freckles appear on the bridge of her nose, her chest and feet are hot, her hair still half-wet from the bath. Her tongue puckers when she sips a tart beer, the can sweating, leaving a ring of condensation on the wood beneath.

Charlie's across the road with the garden hose sprinkling the plants in his stripey shorts. Spider webs glimmer in the late-day sun, dandelion puffs float lazily by, and it's Sunday, 6:48 p.m.

I'd love it

we have a song,
and it's a little rough
around the edges,
uncomfortably dark
but brimming with
senseless optimism
(like us.)
and I listen
to it obsessively,
infectious madness
filling emptiness, and I
am smiling helplessly,
winter air rushing in
open truck windows,
picturing you beside me,
your hands all over me,
veering toward traffic,
overcorrecting last minute,
driving off the shoulder,
laughing hysterically.
pulled over, tangled limbs,
backseat steam, kissing
endlessly like we're 15.
you make me feel
everything, especially
fear that you are
precisely what I need,

fear that I would
destroy you or you me.
fuck it, though —
I love the danger of it.
we only have another
sixty years or so, if
we're that cursed or lucky.
our graves are already
digging themselves.
and I want you now,
careless and free,
tying me to a tree
and having your way
with me.
and I'm not sure
if I've ever been fully in it,
or if I've ever really made it,
but if we did, well —
I think you know
how I'd feel about it.

weak and complete

Mid-afternoon in a darkened room, his rhythmic breath the only audible sound as he drifts serenely into slumber. His dreams are perhaps graced by my presence, freshly inspired by sins just committed.

And I am not tired, but at peace nonetheless. Perched across the room on a chaise, bare-legged sipping whiskey. My throat is raw from the force of his hands around it and I smile indulgently at the memory. Between these legs I ache, raw from taking him for so long while somehow craving more of him at once.

But I will let him sleep. I will be patient as I wait for him to patch the insatiable void in me. And he does — God, in the moment I forget my own name. I forget anything that ever once meant anything and he is everything. His mouth hovers longer on my scars, and when he exhales against my lips I feel him resuscitate parts of me I had once pronounced dead.

And I can see it in his eyes when he's underneath me. That blind adoration, the release of control to me, the way he almost forgets his rough ways and makes love to me face to face. And I have no desire to tame him, only to keep him here in this place he tells me he hasn't been.

I light up a cigarette and embrace its familiar noxious taste. I may still love to dance with the idea of death but I have never felt more alive. The fabric of his shirt soft against my skin, the single candle flickering, his masculine frame exposed from above the waist, his arm draped overhead.

I find myself rushing through the cigarette, downing the last swig of whiskey before making my way to bed. Quietly slipping beneath the sheets, the first touch of his skin warm on mine. He stirs and presses all of me to him, and with his arm draped heavily over me I am weak though somehow in this instant complete.

And I wonder idly if this is what love is.

too much

You write about love too much.

Maybe it's because I've never been in it deep enough. I dip my feet in and it's cold, and I've never liked being cold, and everyone's shouting from the deep end, 'come on, it's warm once you're under, get in!' But I can't. I'm shivering, standing alone on the sand in the wind, waiting for the perfect stranger, knight with skin like armour, to toss me over his shoulder and carry me in.

You think about sex too much.

The lines of sex and love are powdery and blurred. I snort both at once and get high on the drug. They fuck me, then they love me. It's not a coincidence. And in the end, we all just want to be loved, don't we?

Don't we?

And I love that they do, and I love being the muse, the perfect woman, but it's not enough, it's never enough.
When I have them I leave and long to be lusted for by some other man (especially a seemingly unattainable one again). And I've never felt fire the way I imagine it when

I'm all alone and hot and bothered and sensual and creative. That breathless, soul-consuming, sin-absolving, roof-on-fire thing I'm after.

Is it you? Is it him?

Searching and trying and still not finding, and I really ought to be more careful but I'm a ticking time bomb dying to detonate, so what do you expect?

You talk about your mental illness too much.

Thanks for noticing. What were your parents like? Did you grow up privileged? Did you always have a ton of friends? Have you ever been beaten and sucked dry? It must be nice to have well-oiled neurons. It must be easier not to have to swallow 5 pills and your trauma every morning when you wake up nauseous. It must be nice not to spin. Not to have to choose between numbness and raging emotion. Is it? I wouldn't know, and never did.

You're too delicate, too complicated, too much.

And you fucking bore me.

what's meant to be

you wanted me to write something,
so you used a lethal weapon —
silence.

it's a dull ache,
a heaviness tainting every breath,
because I thought for a second
that it might feel right
laying on a cheap mattress,
watching Netflix,
drinking expensive beer
and spilling out dreams
of conquering the world,
even if we might be
in the working class forever.

we could have climbed mountains,
laughed too much,
and lay in bed listening
to country songs
and breath and heartbeats,

but I'll keep telling myself
what's meant to be
will be.

ecstasy

and for this,
I don't want a trace
of alcohol on my lips.
I don't want to be drowsy.
I want to drown you
in my energy.
I don't want the memory
of this night to be hazy.
I want to play it back
again and again,
tomorrow, years later,
like a favourite record.
eyes closed, transfixed
again by the ecstasy,
the unmatched pleasure
of your hands on my body.
an answered prayer
and a mortal sin.
the end of me,
and where I begin.

held inside

The future is bleak, so I'm taking a week, if only to sleep deep in the sand on a lonely beach, endeavor to teach myself to breathe again, remembering days when it didn't ache, when I didn't fake smiles or count tiles just to kill time, just to rhyme word with heard the words spoken.

Guess I'm broken — always was though, so it's hard to know if I'm really hurt worse, or if there's a curse I've cast upon myself. Yet no one else is to blame, and I came to no logical conclusion, fed a plausible delusion, lost the truth with my youth somewhere, and you don't have to care, it's fine — this mess is mine, and I'm too tired to clean it.

Didn't mean to demean it, whatever it was. Felt the buzz before the climax, saw the I-Max, silver screen, wet dream, nightmare, to be fair, I never pay attention.

Always loved the tension, spanning vast expanses, entertaining last chances, stealing sidelong glances, demanding sultry dances to and fro.

And who could know the extent of pent-up damage? No bandage, just a gash. Thrash and gnash at anyone who tries to tongue the wound, wholly consumed by this dissonance, and since no one asked, I'm tasked with the duty to strip the beauty away, reveal the real deal underneath that I sheath at times — poorly executed crimes and I'm guilty as charged.

Barged through the gates for no reason. Call it treason. Call it wrong. I don't belong out of harm's way. What can I say, except no one knows the half of it?

So laugh at it. Ignore it. Tell me you're bored of it. Shout profanities, predict calamities, carve a notch or stop and watch me spurt this ink in the bathroom sink. Watch me pour out all over the floor till the well runs dry and I finally die.

Don't speak. Don't be weak. Lay me down. Let me rest. Don't compress this mottled chest. Dismember me, and remember please, to rip out the heart and slice it apart if only to see what it held inside — and let that remain between you and I.

red-handed

it's been a slice.

when you sliced me open,
poetry spilled out,
splattering all over
silk bedsheets,
gliding in neon hues
across brick walls,
trickling slowly
from temple
to cheek to lips,
a single drop
falling on you,
feeling it, wet,
sweat on your jaw,
watching me move
in awe.

it's hard to say
whose hands
are more crimson,
because
when you caught me
red-handed,

threw me
up against the wall,
our fingers
were intertwined
the whole damn time.

you have the luxury
of letting this fade,
and I'll let you,
won't regret
what I felt with you.
you prefer things
that are rational.
you choke
on I love you's
while I scream
about you
on mountaintops
and treat you
like a god.

it must be nice
not to feel this much,
I mean, I know
I'm kind of fucked,

but I fall asleep at night
knowing I've chased
every whim and dream,
and you admire
the way I think,
but you don't
have it in you.

nice knowing you.

before I lose myself

Call me. Call me at midnight or nine in the morning. Come and find me before I lose myself.

There's no embellished way to say it. I'm lonely.

And I can't bear another wasted day to myself. I don't know what I'm living for when not loving someone else.

Call me weak but I only need to be held. Strong arms engulfing me night till morning. The closeness, the heat of another pressed against me.

I can't stare any longer at the walls or the paintings. I can't listen to the wind and the rain and the house creaking. Shivering. Withering beneath these blankets.

I need distraction. Languid passion. To be kissed for hours on end without expectation and told 'we have all the time in the world.'

Legs entangled, head pressed to bare chest, thudding heart, warm breath. Fingers raking rhythmically through messy hair.

Sweet nothings that are everything. Falling asleep smiling.

To give myself away. To trust. To rest peacefully. To release the love that rages within me.

To know someone and allow them to know me.

To love away the lonely.

a poet's bed

he's sitting there at his typewriter, frowning,
warm light shining on the silver in his hair,
left leg restless, fingers tapping,
taking a long sip of scotch on the rocks, savouring.
and I'd like to tear him away from his writing,
but tonight I don't pull my usual trick
of walking past him without pants.
I just watch him
from the warmth of his king bed,
unable to focus
on the Hemingway I've been reading.

and I might be the muse tonight — oftentimes I am.
but perhaps, it's an ex,
or a woman he met at the farmer's market,
or it might be that outlaws and pirates
have taken hold of him again.
or perhaps it's a poem about eating breakfast,
but I'll devour it, whatever it is, when he finishes.
I'll get a glimpse inside that brilliant mind,
peruse the libraries within, drink the mystery of him,
his hands all over me as I read him, ready
for another sleepless night in a poet's bed.

glitch

you're the rush of dopamine
flooding my basal ganglia,
the longing and the reward;
the stray thought that became
an irreversible glitch
in my orbitofrontal cortex,
fixed on you down
to a neuronal level.

it's a different kind of fever —
the kind that leaves you hot
in all the right places.
sinus tachycardia all over
my electrocardiogram,
respiratory acidosis
when you come too close
and I forget to breathe.

we ought to find a place
to talk about sensation.
teach me all you know
about fine, discriminative touch
and proprioception.
watch me come alive
in the perception, infection,
sweet paresthesia.

we keep on writing volumes
of unintentional erotica
every time our eyes meet,
lips part, breath catches.
I find myself fantasizing about
your mouth on mine,
your rough hands tangled up
and pulling on my hair.

spasms and convulsions,
tension and depth,
lost awareness and
the ache of overstimulation.
oxytocin drawing out tears of relief
that fall on flushed cheeks,
fingertips examining my back,
counting my vertebrae.

naughty neural circuits,
always sizzling and sparking,
causing exponential
excitatory postsynaptic potentials
in the mind
of a hot, restless mess
with a weakness for adrenaline
and the way it feels to want you.

lucky you

I will immortalize you
in these tear-stained pages,
and your great-grandchildren
will blow the dust from
this antique cover
and read of how
I felt for you -
the man I
couldn't
have.

bloodthirsty

you stand statuesque
in the crosshairs
of my machine gun heart,
hands in the air,
surrendering
to an inevitable death.

I am too bloodthirsty
tonight to spare
a wanted man like you.
you smile,
my finger presses
heavier on the trigger,

did you want to grab a drink with me?

... boom.

you win

I'm happy for you,
with your golden life,
with your smiling eyes,
and your beach trips
and birthday parties.

I don't know you,
though from afar,
you seem to have
lucked out
in this draw of life.
you seem to have won
the 6/49,
or at least
the encore.

I don't hear
about the fights,
the nights
you sleep
downstairs
with the TV on,
the days
you can barely
drag yourself
in to work.

I bet you are
saddled with
responsibilities,
and sometimes
you wish you had
some time alone
to drink too much
and make bad decisions.
still, I think
you have it
better than I do,
because although
I am young
and relatively free,
I like to hold myself
underwater in the bath,
and imagine dying
covered in bubbles,
and sometimes
I drive too close
to 18-wheelers
on purpose.

the world has its way
of faulting me
for my honesty.

people like to criticize
the way I spill truth,
calling down to me
from comfortable perches,
telling me they're worried,
telling me to lie more,
to sugarcoat these words.
but I have no desire
to be labelled 'sweet.'
I am what I am,
and I'll always
find myself
wrapped up
in some sort
of misery,
but at least
I'm not a liar
or a cheat,
and at least
I don't pretend
that everything
is alright
when it is
absolutely
fucked.

cold-hearted

Find the void and fill it. Pack the gash with anything that fits. Fuck or drink the pain away if there is any — if in your eyes, it meant anything.

Forget it. And don't forgive it — not ever. I do infatuation well and cold-hearted better. In a melodramatic world such as this where all we have are words and false appearances, we can hide any filthy truth we like. No one is exempt.

Against all odds, we cage stars within our eyes, dying to believe in far-fetched realities. Imaginations impractical and running rampant. Numbness laid to fleeting rest in a shallow grave, burying it with just enough hope to hide its ghastly blue face.

But it is ever-present, gnawing through stomach walls and palpitating ventricles. And I've not known the alternative to crashing and burning. These hands much like Midas' but simply incinerating, unless the object was somehow fireproof to begin with.

Pensively, I endeavor to make myself feel something, but when blown this finicky fuse is not receptive to any form of fixing.

Once-flooded lands parched as the drought arrives. There is no rain in my soul to bring this garden back to life.

Forever weaving narratives of a picturesque life, yet feigning to mention I'm dead inside.

smoke rings (one night with you)

If you're looking for me, which, I'm betting you won't be, you can find me blowing smoke rings, foolishly hoping you'll call to say you read me wrong — dyslexic. That I made you feel electric. That you belong in the lyrics of a country song next to me on this rickety porch, talking about anything half the night, warily eyeing the white spider and its elaborate web, knowing when we tire we'll retire to that king bed and make love or fuck all over again.

Call it what you want to. I only know I want you tonight. I never said you were the rest of my life, but I can't say I'd have been against it. I knew it when our eyes met, drinking on that riverbed.

You fill my sorry head with questions of how you left burn marks rather than impressions and how one night with you without the promise of two has me bordering on depression.

I never smoke this much. Thinking of your touch, I end up drinking myself numb, unsure how to crawl out from underneath your thumb.

I've been under men before in order to get over them. A one-night rush designed to flush them from my system.

I didn't give myself to you with that intention. Was the chemistry intense, or was it all my invention?

You're busy. You're dizzy. You're spinning. Luck or a lack thereof threw a wrench in our plans but these hands aren't afraid of getting filthy, and if you let me, I'll twist your bolts until they come free, implore you to see what you don't believe you need. Watch me bleed.

And it's desperate. It's obsessive. It's borderline aggressive. I should quit while I'm behind, but perhaps the worry in your mind has shaken you. Overtaken you.

And I wish I could be there for you, but apparently my presence feels too relentless for you to entertain me, and if ever you read this I'm certain you'll think I'm fucking crazy, but how many women have you met who really let you get inside their head?

I'll be dead before I'm dishonest, and isn't that what you said you wanted? She lied and cheated, and I wish you could see it, but these eyes and this bleeding heart have hyperfocused on you. I move too fast — that much is true. But you ought to take responsibility for being the riptide to whisk me off to sea. There never was much hope for me.

As my head submerges beneath your surface, my lungs fill with your memory. I know it's over, and I'll learn to accept it, but I haven't come to terms with the term 'rejected'.

It's hard to look at those sheets where your body fit to mine like a missing piece. It's easier to think this story will be continued than to accept its melancholy ending.

You're free, and easy, and probably better off without me. But on the off-chance you change your mind and make it timely — you know exactly where to find me.

I'll be blowing smoke rings, imagining things that will never be.

Or are you out there tonight still thinking of me?

the long way home

late evening drives
on two-lane roads
by the river,
windows down,
lilac air blowing in.
overgrown boys
speeding past
in wheezing cars,
old people on bikes
struggling over
the little hills,
daredevil birds
dancing near
truck wheels.
trees drowning
out on the point,
the channel surface
like glass.
sunbeams sparkling
on metal mailboxes,
hand resting
by the side mirror,
waving in the wind,
tapping the door.

smile spreading
on thin lips,
free from
the thoughts,
for once —
just feeling.

possession

contorting
and convulsing
underneath you,

demons exiled
temporarily...

(they'll be back.)

leave me dreaming

My dreams are never lucid. A narrative far beyond my control, a smooth country drawl flooding the background of the scene played out, and I cannot close my eyes even if the sight is one that leaves me with a gouging ache when I eventually wake.

Four wooden walls dim in the absence of sunlight. Comforting darkness. Crickets chirping intermittently. The shrill call of a loon somewhere in the distance. Windows open. Breeze lifting thin curtains gently. Old building shifting, creaking. The scent of lilacs carried in. Breathing it in, sighing deeply.

Sweat on my skin, blankets heavy. Intense humidity. Dusk fast approaching. Small shelter shrouded in darkness. Safety in these walls. Enveloping silence, save for the sound of trees and nocturnal creatures. Soothing song of surfacing frogs. Lonesome coyote howling. Full moonlight dripping in, landing on our skin.

Finger tracing my lips — they fall open. Your touch gentle, following the faint light on my face, watching the way it reflects in pools of ink. You say you could spend the night just watching me. Hands patient, leisurely.

Leaving me in agony. Sheets more tangled than our limbs. A desperate ache hanging in the air with the heat. My heart screams:

Know me fully. Carve your name into my throat with your teeth. Make me wild. Capture and release me. Bleed for me. Say the words that catch in your throat with conviction, then say them over and over again. Redefine what love is. Give me something I'll never find again. Destroy me. Piece me together slowly. Flood me. Nourish me. Eviscerate me. Pledge allegiance to my demons. Be true to me or leave me dreaming.

embers

does it burn a little
that I am not
burning for you?

our flames have waned;
the glowing embers
of my fading attention
are all that remains.

we smoldered once,
birthed thick smoke
without fully igniting.

and we never will,
but I will stoke
this fire again
when I can,

throw another man
on this skin-searing bed,
consume him ruthlessly

till only
his ashes
are left.

growing pains

Do you remember when you were young, and you lay in bed restless on summer nights, waking with your legs aching, crying into the sheets, rubbing your calves listlessly before drifting off to another haunting dream?

There is pain now, but you feel it deep in your abdomen. A dull, persistent ache that you try and fail to shake. Your bones are no longer lengthening. Your faulty circuits are what need changing.

It's the belief that you were broken from the beginning, the idea that you deserve the agony you're in. You grew too fast when you were young, your shoulders held so much for someone so young and they are weak now and it is hard some days even to hold your head up.

You honed the parts of you that care for others, you gave and gave but you forgot to leave anything for yourself, and now you are hollow and hungry. You guilt yourself for the patterns you've created, you can hardly stand to be alone in a room with yourself because when you look in the mirror you hardly recognize the woman there. She is tired and tense and she has seen too many ghosts — her suffering is palpable.

And it hurts to be all alone with your twisted thoughts and to see at once all the beautiful possibilities melded with destructive tendencies, the rise you get from killing yourself slowly, the tormented creature constantly seeking approval from anyone that will throw it around, never knowing that any number of compliments or kisses or candid conversations will not fill the void or mend the wound. That rather than looking outward for answers, they lie somewhere in your trembling heart.

You ought to stop being a martyr and put the oxygen mask on yourself instead of holding it for someone else whose breath comes slow and easy as your lips turn blue and you succumb to another unnecessary death.

You were never seen for what you were, and so now you expose yourself unabashedly to the masses. You wear your heart and your mind on your sleeve, you have a depth that puts the ocean to shame and when you love, you spare nothing — you are a hurricane.

You are a wildflower, fragile though enduring. I see you rising when the sun burns you and the wind bends you and the rain drowns you. Amidst the pain, here you are — growing.

lakeside musings

you'd have loved it.
eyes flickering open at dawn
to the solemn music of a loon calling,
the lake still and lavender-grey,
fog hanging heavy in the air
with the promise of a humid day,
and the purr of an antique motor.
sprawled in a wooden boat,
sunburnt lips tracing a bottle neck,
stray water droplets defining
the lines of sun-kissed hips,
legs dangling over the edge,
bracing for the thrill
of uncharted waters.

the nerve

alone on a balcony again,
vibrant winter starlight
blurred by misty eyes,
smoking a menthol cigarette
in a burgundy party dress,
bare shoulders shivering,
pale skin shimmering,
carefully contemplating
ditching the stilettos
and climbing up on the railing.
wouldn't that be a scene.
but no one wants to clean
blood and guts off the street
on Christmas Eve.

the door swings open.
two laughing figures appear,
interrupting my twisted reverie,
spilling their drinks clumsily,
colliding too feverishly to notice me.
fucking ridiculous.
I curse their blissful ignorance,
extinguish the cigarette,
blink back the tears,
paint the fake smile on my lips,

and venture back inside,
into the tipsy crowd, the light.
maybe by New Year's Eve
I'll find the nerve to die.

fragile mind

I was born a week late. A fleetingly blissful unencumbered state. And I posit I was somehow cognizant of, and hesitant to stand at the helm of the pressures awaiting in the external realm.

Fragile mind hardwired to be eternally uneasy. Perpetually queasy with worry, I hurry from one objective to the next, never rest, plagued with a restless heart, its cartilaginous cage insufficient to contain existential rage.

Wondering, blundering blindly, my arrival untimely and departure prearranged, mind perpetually unchanged, aching and longing yet never belonging, searching for meaning, occasionally gleaning self-awareness, though nonetheless I continue my destructive path, merciless wrath inflicted both upon myself and those who come too close.

I damage and dose myself apathetic. They never get it. Lukewarm hands and balanced minds telling me that everything will be fine, but I don't fucking believe it.

Half-love it and leave it the way it did me. It could never see to my depths, and yes, I ascertain I am the Marianas Trench to their barrel of rain. Pleasure and pain, but mostly the latter. What does it matter in the end? Never moan nor bend these days.

A fog, a haze, ample time to overthink, abandoning smoke and drink for painful reflection, solitary dejection. Need a new plan, need a new man, need something to make me fucking feel again.

Latency, complacency, wait and see, perhaps there'll be a less miserable chapter, reasonably happily ever after all.
Fall, crawl and fucking break. Have your cake and eat your words, and fuck what you've heard inside your mind. Perhaps you'll find something worth holding, for once not folding before the game begins.

Wake me up in sixty years and tell me who wins.

filthy

you imagine
dainty hands,
fingernails piercing biceps,
legs wrapped delicately
around your waist,
moving you gently,
sentimentally,
no.

I will fuck with you
till your skin burns raw,
till you gasp
and scream for mercy,
teeth clenching,
body bending,
begging for
my filthy mouth
on your skin.

I am not
the woman
you think I am.
I will drill into your bones
and drink your marrow
like it's gin.

I tell the moon

I tell the moon about you
when your words escape me,
when you succumb
to vivid dreams of me —
arcing involuntarily and
consuming you as ruthlessly
as my eyes have had you imagining.

a curled catastrophe,
bleary-eyed in the driver's seat,
haunting a vacant parking lot
with my pensive presence,
pondering our trajectory —
emotional lability coupled
with loyal propensities.

I tell the moon about you
and he blushes, hiding his face
with a cloud momentarily.
he tells me every wound
must bleed before healing,
and roads worth travelling
are never paved smoothly.

happiness looks unusual,
though beautiful on me,
and my pursuit of something
otherworldly is ambitious,
and unlikely as success may be,
he admires the way my mind
drifts to brighter galaxies.

I tell the moon about you
late at night while you sleep.
I tell him you perplex me,
and I want only to learn you,
and keep you a mystery.
and he tells me you say
the same things about me.

on the beach alone

I sit on the beach alone,
watching the couples,
insecure together,
standing in waist-deep water,
having shitty conversations
about nothing.

I am on my oversized towel
on the dry grass next to the sand,
reading Bukowski,
and I think he makes me feel
a tad more judgmental
than usual.

the sweat collects
on the small of my back
and I stand, sailor-striped one-piece
halfway up my ass.
I keep my thick sunglasses on
and saunter to the water.

I wonder what
those sad fuckers
are thinking of me.

I see the women subtly scowling,
clutching their husbands,
knowing they're looking.

I wonder if any of them
wish they were single.
I wonder if they envy me —
the only one here alone,
the only one reading
and sitting quietly.

I am content now,
with my brown shoulders
and my poetry books,
and a figure I don't work for.
I'd rather be a little lonely
than entirely miserable.

like the leaves

we walk beneath
a golden canopy,
fingers interlaced,
shoulder to shoulder,
air biting our cheeks.
threads of sunlight
weaving between branches,
gravel road dead,
only silence ahead —
a dreamlike
autumn paradise.

slowing our pace,
we find ourselves
pressed together,
chest on pounding chest,
the laugh lines
around your eyes deepening,
hands hovering
on the small of my back,
dancing slowly
to the sound
of the breeze,
and like the leaves,
I find myself falling
helplessly at your feet.

parallel lines

meet me
in the middle —

somewhere between
logic and madness,
intimacy and indifference,
benevolence and bitterness.

we have been stumbling
blindly on a darkened path,
parallel lines never touching,
a distant coexistence.

show me the way
to you again.

fluorescent wasteland

here we stand again
in this fluorescent wasteland,
projecting false narratives,
vomiting empty promises,
if only because we can.
you call me old-fashioned
for seeking a natural remedy
for the poison circulating
through my half-eaten veins,
but this free-for-all mentality
has become disenchanting,
demeaning, demanding —
a fairground full of freaks
wearing masks of normalcy.
selling a few hundred copies
of our carefully fabricated,
exaggerated stories,
burying our thirst for sex
in shallow graves,
skeletal hands emerging
from beneath borrowed creativity
and the dirty pursuit of fame.
and I partake in it, I must say,
but this is not all of me.
this is merely a hobby.

I'm quite aware
it likely always will be.
I earn every cent I make,
and few can relate to the drive
for something more
burning me alive at my core.
I am so much more
than what I let you see of me,
and I am not so desperate
for a pair of hands on my body
that I will sacrifice my dignity.
I am a whispered secret,
unheard amidst the resounding
screams for validation.
I already know
I look good with the lights on.
I already know
I can achieve anything alone.
I am already everything
I ever once dreamed
someone else would be for me.
I am far from desperate
for anything you can offer me,
and I bet that's a little intimidating.

blind

even if I were blind,
I'd still have fallen for your mind.

trust issues

you were
an accident
from the get-go,
and so,
there is
a part of you
that doesn't trust
the world
when it tells you
you are loved.

someone
can shower you
in affection,
and yet,
still,
you wonder
if they really
care,
or if they just
feel obligated to.

poets and pain

you're a poet,
artist,
gypsy.
you bleed
neon words
and glitzy lyrics.

when the going
gets too good,
you rustle up
some pain.

you write
when you feel,
and when you feel
anything intensely,
it's one part ecstasy,
two parts agony.

Charles and Ernest
and all your other
tortured heroes
did not lead
peaceful lives,
yet here you are again
trying on their shoes.

you talk about
your mangled soul
like its fate
is well beyond
your control,
like it's all already
been decided.

but you know
damn well,
you do this
to yourself.

ethereal erythropoiesis

I bleed exceptionally —
cutthroat carotid carving.
slit, slick and spurting,
hemorrhaging words.
I want you.
no one else will do.
coaxing the wound,
my hands and the tiles
burgundy, lips blue.
dying to drain
these delicate veins,
but they find a way
to flood the sickly
gnashing organ
within me
just enough that
it carries on beating.
erythropoiesis
ethereal, alarming...
and perhaps
I'd coagulate
if you were
to reach for me,
hemostatic hands
healing.

otherwise,
you ought to be
the death of me,
but you like me
half alive, weak,
needing and bleeding
profusely.

fault lines

There must be truth in the saying 'any attention is good attention.' For I am attuned to your frequency, awaiting anything that may fall freely from your lips, and you pull words from these pieces of me, if only to remind me that you are still listening. That I have not yet vacated your mind.

And I wish I were blind because it hurts to watch you remind her that you're giving her the time. Now more than ever, I might hazard. Absorbing every line she writes and leaving tangible traces of desire in your wake. Do you tell her what you told me? Does she still seem to worry?

We act as pretty patches. I do apologize for playing with matches after bathing in gasoline, and for the way I tend to make a fucking scene. It will end inevitably when we cease to play upon the other's creativity and let the ashes scatter in the breeze.

It will end and begin again when another cynical woman is convinced the weight has lifted, succumbing to the intoxicant, ignoring the fault lines and building dreams upon them. Hurriedly fashioning the walls we all seem to be lacking. Homeless hearts taking shelter in haunted houses, rummaging through closets discovering suits and skeletons. Preparing to carry the bones outside to bury beneath the ever-weeping willow, pruning the vines that strangle and tangle, repainting the walls of the ocean-front house passionately until tragedy strikes.

Whether earthquake or wildfire, tidal wave or meteor, history has shown there is always a greater evil destined to extinguish the lone, hopeful candle. You weren't — but at the least, I prefer to tell myself you wanted to be. (Just let me.)

free association

come to me with your affliction —
a dimly-lit room, the prone position.

couch fabric against your cheek,
a slew of scents to perceive —
cigarette smoke, vanilla icing,
stale bourbon and unapologetic sex.

breathe, and remove the sieve
that snares unconscious thought.

succumb to the quietness,
the absence of distraction,
and the soft, feminine
persuasiveness of my voice.

become a passerby.
translate the language
of the dark side of the mind.

let hysteria and hedonism
reveal their power
amidst latent love stories
and euphemistic eulogies.

unrepentant parapraxis
assists in my analysis,

a Freudian slip
of the tongue that I'll taste
when you're done oversharing —
countertransference.

we ought to do this
every Wednesday.

hippocampus,
hippopotamus.

slap my ass and call me Electra.

there's a certain freedom
in our association.

no mercy

it has to hurt
for her to like it.
think about it.
your teeth around
her bottom lip,
causing it to swell,
grimace morphing
into mirth instantly.
erratic breathing,
hands tightening
around her neck,
exposed, extended,
only lessening
your aggression
when her eyes
start to widen.
lithe little body,
raw and bruised,
arms tethered
above her head
just the way
she likes them.
uninhibited,
animalistic,
gasping
and begging —

never for mercy,
   but rather
   helplessly
   for more.

don't

if you see me in a bookshop,
breathing in the smell of paper,
fingers tracing over the pages
of some lesser-known classic...

if I ask for black coffee
at the café, and like always,
I'm running late
and my hair is messy...

if I'm shooting Patron
at a dive bar mid-week,
slow dancing with a man
you've never seen...

don't look my way,
don't say my name,
don't reach for me.

don't remind me
of everything we used to be.

to know you

You bleed ferocity, and I, intimacy. When it comes to you, I cannot control my impulsivity. The collective ache we feel is more than real as the rain on the tin roof above floods fragile souls with promised love.

I want only to know you. I am brimming with the belief that I might be in every dream locked inside your wild mind, and tonight you are little else but mine.

I come to you dressed only in flickering candlelight. You inhale sharply at the sight. And you may be a man of verse profound but hush... not a sound. There are no words for this. Skin on skin, silencing your breath with an agonizing kiss. And I know your selfless ways. I pin your arms — you resist. With you beneath me, I persist. You have earned this. You deserve this. You are more than a master of sweet deliverance. Lie still and give over to this. My only wish — to give you everything on earth you've ever missed.

With hands light on ivory skin, I begin to learn every longing inch — examining burns and scars and rips, palms coming to rest on anxious ribs. A tranquil silence flooding your existence as I survey the gradual evening of your breath. A wisp of a smile touching your lips as with attentive fingertips I trace feather-light maps across your chest — and perhaps all roads lead to your beating heart, and perhaps this is only the start.

Believe me when I say this — in this bed you will lose sight of your brokenness. To my lips you surrender, as they linger on your neck remember, I will erase every trace of what once might have been enough. You cannot fathom the intensity with which you will now forever long for me, and I, you. Together anew.

Your teeth clenched, our bodies bend to meet the other and I hover, savouring the sight of you wide-eyed and wanting before I release your wrists and you grip my hips and we melt together. I possess you wholly as you hold me, gasping — an instant everlasting.

her

you want a girl
who smells like lemon meringue
and tastes like sour raspberries.

grabs you by the throat
when you're underneath her,
then laughs against your mouth.

sleeps through the rain,
and wakes you on summer mornings,
wanting to drive somewhere, anywhere.

cries when she's angry,
smokes when she's stressed,
drinks to savour the taste.

loses herself in your arms
when she can't calm herself;
trembling and vulnerable.

sings off-key when she bakes,
looks like a hippie or a librarian
depending on the day.

loves your stupid jokes,
bandages your wounds,
makes you feel alive again.

she is a disaster.
her mood changes every five minutes.
her thoughts are chaotic.

young and vibrant,
impulsive and twisted
and damaged.

she wants what she wants,
and right now,
it's you.

ode to dark roast

you warm me
from the inside.
you swim in my throat.
I drink you in greedily,
your scalding sustenance
bitter and harsh on my tongue.
day beginning on the right note,
you go swimmingly with a smoke,
and if I'm honest,
I'd probably slap a bitch
if I didn't have you close.
you're my favourite addiction,
dark-bodied and delicious.
my motivation for waking,
hands shaking, craving
more of you always.
and they say
I need to curb my intake,
but I love the heat you bring
to these ever-frigid hands,
and the way
you make my heart race,
and the way
you taste.

snack

I have an overactive imagination.
it's unsettling, the positions
I've put you in.

a careless touch unleashed
a monsoon of inspiration,
a torrent of sin.

I apologize for what I dreamt of
when I was lust drunk...
can we go back?

I was hungry for a muse,
and you were looking
like a snack.

lies

act like you want me
for the sake of my writing.
mess with me well enough
that I start to use you
for my musings, now-dormant,
hibernating, waiting
for fresh inspiration.
I like to get high on love
in person, but lately,
I'm far too cautious to allow
anyone to hold me for more
than a night and morning,
and there are never
any lasting feelings.
but I'll admit it —
I miss what he did to me,
even if it wasn't right for me,
even if he fucked my mind
into submission and had me
missing a man I hadn't met yet.
we were a psychological thriller
with elements of horror,
plentiful drama and a touch
of romantic comedy,
but by the closing scene
neither of us were laughing.

rather, sitting alone in the dark,
too affected to sleep properly.
reality might be relaxing
and far more healthy,
but I miss the delusions,
the butterflies, the fantasy.
bring it back to me.
keep me up all night.
make me write incessantly,
and tell me ridiculous lies,
like you're falling,
and I'm all you see,
and you love me.

spilled

the words flourish,
grow within
like dandelions
or cancer,
expand,
press themselves
against
my cranial bones,
demanding
to be spilled
onto dimly lit keys
or empty margins.

SELF-DESTRUCT

oh, to be
illogical...

to destroy
one's life

in pursuit
of a feeling.

(this
damned
feeling
again.)

UNWRITTEN

if I said I wanted one weekend,
I'd be lying.
but this is not a declaration of devotion,
an optimistic proclamation.
the image of us holds a certain clarity —
a quiet understanding.
mutual attraction spanning beyond
raw, battered skin.
all I need is you to hold my throat
and my attention.
make me beg for your passion and rage,
then flood me.
don't overthink it when you bury your face
in my hair exhaustedly.
don't resist the magnetic pull of my skin,
or fight the addiction.
liquor on our breath, body and mind
similarly ravaged.
escaping with an ache we can't shake,
and novels unwritten.

please

cigarette smoke and a smirk,
words rolling low, storming.
this man takes my cynicism
and tears it roughly at its seams,
spilling sensual daydreams.
and these cheeks ache from
the grin he colours them with,
tongue longs for his fevered kiss,
and I shudder from deep within,
an emptiness only remedied
by him, and I am
bound and begging,
mind whirling, heart hurting,
bruised throat and knees,
raw and wanting
more pain,
please.

delicate

rip her dress till it falls.
get your claws on her flesh.
taste her life on your lips
as you tear through her chest.

threading fingertips
through
the fifth
intercostal space,

spreading bones
as with curtains,
splattered blood
on your face.

hold her
palpitating heart
in your palm
here at last,

her ventricles
flailing
and failing
her fast.

abating,
deflating,
delicate
breath.

throbbing,
delicious,
imminent
death.

the flowers

I don't understand you,
and maybe I'm not supposed to.
maybe I don't deserve honesty
or candid conversation.

as I swallow the hard pill,
I realize I've been trying to breathe life
into a dead mouth, and if it's goodbye,
I'll miss who you are as a person.

I will not chase or pursue.
I wish only the best for you,
and I'm sorry for the time it's taking
to put an end to these writings.

I'm sorry for not being
who you thought I might,
and I hope you never lose sight
of the hope we resurrected briefly.

I need you to know
that it wasn't all a lie,
and it was never my presence
that caused the flowers to bloom.

you needn't search for healing hands
to apply pressure to the wound,
for everything you seek
exists already in you.

the whisper

I find myself in a lull, and while there are ample words to mull over, they do not form readily without a breathing inspiration.

And though I am often at war with my own anticipation for a change of pace, I am tired of the race to find a home in a heartbeat. Callouses cover my feet from walking this dusty road, and I'll admit that carrying the weight of my own load alone is freeing, and there is familiarity in the fleeing.

I can blather on about my internal experience for days, but it will never compare to the ways in which I am moved by a muse, by a ruse. How I love to be tricked, have my arteries nicked by a careless surgeon, promiscuous flesh and virgin heart hemorrhaging for all to see.

Tell me, am I still a thing of beauty even after they have bled me and my skin is translucent and white, and my eyes, dark as night, are motionless and fixed upon yours, reminding you not to deface my grave, for my soul is depraved and will haunt you vigilantly?

I will be but a small figure at the foot of the bed, watching you sleep next to her — she, who may never make you tremble as I might have in the flesh.

Nonetheless, you will feel me in the wind as a chill climbs your spine and my ghostly limbs intertwine with yours. Pray tell why you dream of angels while fucking whores?

My restless spirit, I fear, is not made for heaven. The deadly sins seven are felt intimately, and I will find some semblance of serenity in the walls you inhabit, wreaking gentle havoc, willing the chimes and swing-set to move on a still day. Eliciting a shudder as the curtains sway to the rhythm I create as I toy with them.

I am audible footsteps on rickety floorboards and I am the door that swings open of its own accord. I am the whisper, the inexplicable breath on your neck.

And though much is uncertain, you will not forget.

made-up man

Half-heartedly, they assure me you're out there somewhere waiting. Yet even if you are, I imagine you aren't pining or saving yourself for me. I imagine you live your life boldly. That your days are full without me. And I wish I could say the same for myself, but if I'm honest with you and anyone else, in your absence I am incomplete and aching. And I grow older and more cynical with each passing day. I find myself questioning your very existence, wondering if I am destined for aloneness despite the untamed love that plagues me, eating me alive from the inside slowly.

I catch glimpses of you in all the wrong places. I saw you last night in the earnest face of a married man who seduces without intent. Who spilled his heart out in the darkness, confessing all his past transgressions. Who values my compassion and opinion on love, despite my inability to stay in it. He, whose eyes and proximity burn holes through this un-held body. Who manages to permeate my dreams, evoking a waking physical longing. Who seems to appreciate me in the moments we speak, but forgets any power of mine entirely when not within an arm's reach.

I feel you when imagining a pair of hands that will never truly touch me. He who sits in quiet rooms with me, apparently immune to the tension he evokes in me.

He who does not comprehend the extent of my desire to stand and slam the door shut and beg for just an hour of his touch, his lips on mine. What remains of my pride and better judgement prevents me from doing this every time the thought crosses my mind. I have already put myself on the line for him, with no reciprocation. He is content in his present reality and I'd like for him to be happy. Realistically, despite the way I exude lust and affection, I may never be a practical investment.

I hear you in the depth of his voice. In the sound of him reading lines he wrote in response to mine. In the distant nature of our connection. In the way the combination of two poetic imaginations allowed for the production of an impossible narrative, a desperate and doomed work of fiction. The addictive nature of mutual inspiration, the opening of hearts allowing trapped light to brightly pervade skeptical minds. The sly, unlikely compulsion to weave hope into the other's writing. I know you in the way I ignored the inconsistencies, blindly mimicking something unconditional, playing house and saying the words I thought had been spoken sincerely, not wanting to imagine they meant anything less falling from his lips than I dreamed.

I fantasize about you when confronted with a more practical possibility. A man within reach, only two years older with arms engulfing and shoulders that have withstood great weight, a man with more to offer than wit or desirability or intelligence.

Someone who might appreciate the extent to which I've struggled to gain what I've attained, someone loyal and consistent with a similar work ethic. Someone I could build a life with. Someone appealing at least on the surface, yet someone I sense holds a great deal beneath it. Someone I'd like to believe might be capable of keeping me. Someone too guarded and responsible to be as impulsive as I tend to be. Someone who may never take a chance on me.

I see pieces of you in all these men. And I am searching, always have been. I imagine I could let one in if it were not one-sided, unrequited. But I pour myself out too readily, too eager to feel a lasting touch, altogether too much. Even if I find you one day, I reckon I'll manage to scare you away. So I remain alone and aching in this bed. As Plath once said, I think I made you up inside my head.

13

I hold my breath
underwater.

63, 64, 65,
why am I still alive?

gasp!

some ghost bitch
with bloody eye sockets
is hanging from the ceiling.

she likes to play
twenty questions

when she isn't
calling me
a fucking coward.

*how many men
have you slept with
altogether?*

good question.
I can't remember.

1, 2 ... 12

do I include
the rapist
in the kill count?

*If you killed him,
I guess.*

13,
& yes.

hanging

I wanted you
hanging
on my every word,
but you slipped
from the noose
unscathed.

use me

you won't deny it
when you're four drinks in,
and I lean in to tell you
I need you and a cigarette,
and my breath is hot
on your flushing neck.

I won't stop you
when you kiss me,
and your hands slide deep
in these blue-jean pockets,
and every inch of you
is pressed against me.

we won't fight it
when my head hits
the brick wall behind me,
and I'm weak and dizzy
(not from the impact)
and I'm tightly wound around you.

you'll understand it
when you see exactly
what it is you do to me,

when we're burning up
your bedsheets and my eyes
are as merciless as my body.

I'll need more of it,
and I'll beg you to use me
until we're raw and you've hurt me,
till you've seen the best and worst of me,
and we decide if what we're left with
is something worth chasing.

the woman rides away

I'm a bad woman,
mad woman,
wreck your heart
and fuck your mind woman.
drowning desperation
in pint glasses,
exhaling silver clouds
of menthol smoke.
casting a line to find
the men bite quick,
and I pull them in
for the hell of it,
catch and release
after sunset.

or sometimes,
I like to keep them
out of their element,
watch them flail around
till they're dead.

I met a man
in a dive bar and said,
'run while you can.'
but he took the barstool
to my right regardless,

and he asked me for
a neon slow dance,
and pretty soon there was
lipstick all over him.

we shut the place down
and made for his cabin.
and the rain made music
on the old tin roof
as he shoved me
against the door,
made love to me on
the living room floor,
and the kitchen table
and the bed.

afterward, we drank
a fifth of whiskey,
smoked on the porch,
and fried bacon.
and we talked about
ghosts and ex-lovers,
and I think I fell asleep
with my head on his chest,
because I dreamt
of his heartbeat.

and in this one I woke up
in his arms and thought,
'I could love him.'
but better to leave now
than whenever I decide
I miss the chase.
better I put these
scuffed boots on,
and take my hat
before it's too late.

in this one,
the woman rides away
at sunrise
on a restless stallion,
her misty eyes
on the horizon,
while the rugged man
with a mess of hair
and raw lips
stands solemnly
in the kitchen,
unable to swallow
a well of feelings.

and she tucks his heart
in her saddlebag
with the others,
not once looking back
as she rides west
toward the next
lonesome town
and cowboy.

starlight

the path we follow is dimly lit,
but glimpses of starlight soothe our starving eyes
as we push forward, trembling,
in the shadow of the cavernous forest.

what we are searching for is undetermined,
but to lose will is to lose all,
so we walk until the bare soles of our feet
are cut and bleeding.

nothing is simple, nothing lacks purpose.

in the brightest of our dreams is a sacred place
where endless sunshine weds the waters of the calmest
pond,
and the shaded branches of a willow by its side
beckon us to take refuge from summer's heat.

we lay beneath, in harmony and peace,
joined wondrously by the lover of our dreams —
that image of perfection we envisioned from childhood.

they lay by our side, their silken touch
lingering on our skin,
with eyes that sear our souls, and lips whose heavenly kiss
melts away every sorrow we've ever felt.

until awakened from this impossible paradise,
we sleepwalk fervently on in the eternal dusk;
a time of neither day or night, love or hatred,
souls or bones,
waiting for an answer we will never find.

a quiet day

let's throw our phones off the bridge
and drive until we find a quiet place
to drink bad wine and smoke cigars
on the riverbank, stare at clouds
and skip stones on the still water.

let's write stories in battered notebooks,
and muse over who we've yet to become.
come with me and leave the noise behind.
taste the intoxicating quiet of mid-May,
and ignore your problems if only for a day.

daily meds

you're a masterful blend
of confidence and awkwardness.
your mask of arrogance
conceals the fragility
tucked beneath your chocolate skin.
I wonder how you taste?
smooth and scalding,
like the dark roast coffee
you constantly sip?
and the knowing smiles,
the lingering closeness
leave me burning
for a midnight tryst that rivals
the vivid dreams of you I've had.
I don't want to take you per os.
I want you intravenously,
mainlined to the heart of me,
your effect felt instantly,
satiating the addict in me.
I don't want you pro re nata.
I want you every morning
and hora somni in my bed.
I'll take my daily meds
in the form of a tall, dark
and handsome jerk from work.

I'll be the patient —
you be the nurse.

plan b

Plan A was much more glamourous. Sensual, attentive sex that ended with the fusion of interlocked bodies, that quivering climax felt intimately by both parties, the sweat on temples and fingernail marks on shoulders, legs wrapped around him refusing to release him from me, indulging in slow, spent kisses. It was optimism and intertwined fingers until reality crept in and I realized there were never any stars in these ebony iris pseudo-skies. The appearance projected was merely a reflection of his.

And when met with a breathing, tangible dose of potential commitment, at long last I found I could not keep it. All these answers I believed existed deep within someone else were only ever present in myself.

For the first time in my life, I see that I am better off alone. For I am difficult, perhaps even impossible to understand. And though I don't expect that anyone will ever comprehend the workings of my mind, I crave it above all else. To be known on another plane of existence. For what makes me tick is not as simple as a collarbone kiss or a tilt of the hips. It's those imaginary eyes that haunt me while gazing deep into mine and seeing me for exactly who I am.

Until then (if ever) I will survive just fine without consistency and affection. I do not need attention.

I desire genuine recognition from a kindred soul. I am fragmented yet still whole. And I can easily swallow a pill and my own hasty decisions without feeling the need to beg the heavens for forgiveness.

I am alone again with my sacred silence and my incessant reflection. I ought to be more cautious, but these days, resorting immediately to plan B doesn't even make me nauseous.

fall

if you think
I fall in love
too easily,

you should
see me

f
a
l
l

out of it.

fusion

I am a woman of romance plagued by prophetic darkness. My mind hovers between idealistic optimism and visions of horrific destruction, whether of myself or of the one I choose to love.

You creep through the trapdoors of my subconscious and sit in the parlour drinking all my vodka. I recall my initial warning. You certainly weren't anticipating there would be a loudspeaker installed in the halls of this charming Victorian house. I yelled into the microphone as you sat startled, sipping and listening.

The funny thing about it was that while you were at my house I had moved into yours and had already begun redecorating (it's going quite well by the way). And while I chain-smoked one evening in your freshly painted bedroom, your distinct drawl blared through the talk radio station I tend to play when the hour is late. And so, in a sobering sermon written for my consumption you told me of your similar appetite for destruction.

Two unfortunate souls whisked together in the same bowl of wicked habits. What would become of us? Would we be infused with eternal bitterness or would our flavours in combination create the sweetest of tastes?

It's hard to say.

My feet remain colder than yours despite you being the one often standing outside in the bitter chill of the night. If we chose to close the distance, if you were to gaze upon these onyx planets without a screen between, perhaps they would truly feel seen.

And were these longing legs wrapped around you, I would feel more a wife than a widow. But my desire to wholly consume you remains pervasive, abrasive. And if I were to sketch paths along your skin you would fall to ruin within my spinning web of seduction, unaware of which direction you were ever even headed.

Perhaps in time we might coalesce, fashioning together our own system of measurement — for I've never quite understood the miles you speak of, and the meter of your rhyme sometimes escapes me.

Locked lately within your pulsating prison, I wonder if doing the time might be more advantageous than wasting it. All this rumination, anticipation, and all I need is a quiet room curled against you, silently synchronically spellbound.

Despite the harshness of the elements and the ominous blackness, we may find in one another a lightness, an absence of gravity in a world so heavy, transcending nature's every law with our ethereal fusion.

With hushed lips and a bleeding pen I dream we are more than a happy illusion.

cedar and smoke

follow her taillights to the mountains.
dust trail spiraling to the summit,
midsummer sky painted in shades
of scarlet and tangerine,
sun a floating orb on the horizon.
surrounded by the almost-silence,
save for twigs snapping underfoot,
a mournful owl calling out to no one,
beginnings of a fire smoldering
as she gathers firewood in the forest,
mouth sealed shut, your eyes
following her movements intently.
chill of dusk permeating the air,
heavy blankets on the ground.
cross-legged woman
with wild hair and warm cheeks,
gentle breeze on your neck.
snapping of the rising flames,
beer moistening your lips,
as she leans on you, breathing in
the scent of cedar and smoke.

heliocentric heartache

I am but a planet
to your sun;
orbiting obediently.

I fear the eclipse
when the moon
separates us
and I cannot
look upon you
even from afar.

you warm me,
but we'll never be close.

(x)

You've been writing a thesis on my body language, analysing the method to my madness.

Your dark brow furrows. Your mouth is set and wrinkled at the corner. You're scribbling formulas on the chalkboard trying to solve for (x).

(My spirit is broken but my heart has a depth that spans beyond that parameters of any calculation. If you love me right, I'll follow you to the ends of the universe into the infinite ever-expanding space).

You'll figure it out.

My dark hair lifts in the wind and my eyes flutter when I speak of my accomplishments. I find it hard to maintain steady eye contact, for fear all the fragile truths will become visible.

I find solace in winding roads and the warmth of the sun and eyelids closed, bath water pouring, the soft serenade of a man's voice reaching me from the radio.

Seeing the best in everything is often a curse. I get caught in dangerous daydreams, imagining the sweet beginnings of stories that are bound to include chapters of pain.

You are the essence of all my hopeful fiction.

When you draw close, I breathe in the sandalwood smell of forever. You take a stethoscope and place it hesitantly on bare skin to auscultate my arrhythmia. Our eyes are full of pent-up promises.

Your fingertips tangle in my hair and I become syncopal. You catch me when I fall and begin to understand. Every touch brings forth an exhalation, all the tension escaping my body as I wordlessly place every facet of my being in your hands.

Your eyes widen and your breath catches when the truth comes forth from the haze.

Perfectly shattered with the pieces in place. The little girl with wide brown eyes glancing at the happy families; the teenager ruminating on hateful words with a knife to her wrist over the kitchen sink; the tired woman chain-smoking at the marina, watching the sun dip below the horizon.

Pouring out like a waterfall time and again, leaving myself bone-dry. Cross-legged on a balcony wishing on falling stars for a torrential kind of rain.

If I could wake up in your arms each morning, I could use mine to shelter the world.

If you were my candlelit bedroom, I could light up the sky.

Feel it and breathe it. Tell me you're the missing link that renders me unbreakable.

I'll be your sweetest dream, your darkest fantasy, your muse.

I'll give you everything on earth.

Wherever you are, just give me you.

not close enough

I hate the small talk.

I know we are
only scratching
the surface of
who we really are,
and your mouth might
force itself to smile,
but your eyes
are holding back.

and when I ask you
how you are,
I want a real answer,
but you give me
the same one
everyone else gets.

and we are not
close enough
for you to pour
your heart out to me,
but I am dying
to get past
these hello's,

to get to the part
where it's you and I
laying ourselves out
for one another,
like forgotten artwork
that will finally be seen.

marbles

we all have our struggles,
and chances are
you have felt far worse than I
ever have or will.
and it's selfish
of me to spill my darkness
out like this,
and let it roll around
like marbles
on the kitchen table.
but I am uncomfortable,
constantly questioning myself.
can you tell?
is the sorrow
in my eyes palpable?
do my lips quiver
when I force them to smile?
is it blatantly obvious
how much I hate myself?
feeble little body,
neurotic neural circuitry,
bastard blood
coursing through me,
the fact that
everything is temporary.

can't feel unwanted
if it's always me leaving.
will you miss me?
yes is an answer
I'll never believe.

this breath

The 18th is approaching, and existential crises are encroaching, and I'm 'still so young,' but I'm not, and one of these years you'll stop saying that. And there are silver hairs tucked in a patch beneath the brown, and I drown in the ocean of my own unmet expectations with next to no hesitation because this wasn't how it was supposed to go.

We all know I wanted 21 with a wedding ring. Creaky floorboards in a fixer-upper farmhouse with a front porch swing. I wanted glowing and growing, my delicate body overtaken by the life held within me. I wanted 'never go to bed angry,' and daybreak kisses and fallen star wishes.

Instead, I lay awake with unfortunate dreams tangled in my head, spread-eagled on a leather couch in an eclectic apartment above a dive bar, with any man who piques my interest so far away, either ambivalent or hundreds of miles distant.

And there are so many steps to take that I doubt I will ever make proper use of the internal fuel that propels my bursting ventricles to duel with logic and reason, committing treason, convincing my skeptical psyche to indulge in the vivid images that keep it ticking in spite of every daunting implausibility lying dormant in my forebrain.

I've had everyday things and discount rings. I've lived a life full of maybes, but I can't resist placing 'the one' before stability and babies. And perhaps 'the one' is only ever 'the many' but I haven't loved any who oscillated at my frequency or had the decency to meet me far above the earth or spent sleepless nights cherishing the explosive devotion I fear is slowly perishing.

I am getting older, and my heart is growing colder, and I am tired of reining in my crazy in a world so hazy. The air is thick and clouded with carcinogenic smoke, and I choke on it and the angst within me, and I'm not sure whether my battered lungs or broken heart will be the death of me, but I am breathless and reckless and full of longing and it all makes me anxious and I wish someone would jump with me because I am tired of crawling up from the bottoms of canyons after being shoved to what many assume will be my death.

This breath is really all I have left.

solutions

I have been living in a dream world
rampant with empty validation.
disconnected from reality,
there are no people around me
because I push them away readily.
and is this what my life is?
25 years old, eyes glued to a screen,
waiting for a message
that might excite me,
a prisoner to these four walls
and technology.
I want to break every screen
and heart
that was never mine anyway.
I have my phone and my men
on a 2-year bring-it-back contract,
and what do I really own in the end?
a truck, medicine, restlessness,
anxiety and depression, debt,
a compulsion to work myself to death,
a heart that hasn't learned to trust yet.
I could use some real friends,
but I am a lonely woman.
always floating, never tied
to anything, always leaving.

and I fake-smile, small-talk,
because most can't handle
a real conversation with me.
and I'm bitching about
my problems again to anyone
awake to like and listen.
forgive me for my negativity.
I am overtired and my life
is a fucking mess again,
but I seem quite well,
so no one will bother
asking how I'm doing.
they'll just tell me their problems
and expect solutions,
but the only solution
I can get down with lately
is beer (a whole lot of it),
so I'll just tell you
to go fuck yourself,
and crack open another can.

in the darkness

We used to write to one another. Ink-fueled confessions and optimistic dreams. A bond forged poetically, of which you were the first and only. A closeness intensified by creativity. You wouldn't know or believe for that matter that it still means anything to me, but as I type these lines I hear the ghost of you reading heart-wrenching prose, and my eyes close, and I half-pretend I'm in that parking lot again.

Since then, you have purged yourself of me, and while it's salt on the wound, I understand completely. I'm only left with the question of whether the action is as easy as you've made it seem, or if you're simply trying to mask what I still mean.

If it were only ever art, you would be proud of it. You would leave your bleeding letters exposed on pages and it wouldn't hurt to remember I was part of your experience or that there were ever moments of honesty and romance. Keep your aura of darkness and project it to the masses, for I still believe gentler parts of you exist even as you may be denying them.

I don't blame you for much of anything. I had conditions and lost faith in the narrative we used to indulge in of making it. And despite my obvious flaws, I was never faking it.

It was real, despite the element of fantasy I seem to splash onto everything.

Too far and too fast, and just because it didn't last doesn't mean nothing will. What a thrill it was, and I often reminisce about the high, the laugher. It's a chapter I won't rip out, even as I learn to live without a flame.

I am not ashamed of what I felt once, or the lines I wrote, or the hope you tore out of me, however temporary it might have been. I'd make a fool of myself all over again if it meant feeling something so intensely. My emotions get the best of me and even if I suffer immensely, I prefer it this way.

I will not repress or forget. Erase your lines, but I will keep your memory in mine. Keep me in the darkness, don't breathe my name again, don't allow the thought of me to move your trembling pen. But remember me quietly in time, and know that I too have not forgotten you.

fooled

when I set my next fire,
I will stand in it
long enough to feel
the flames on my skin.
the burns that remain
on my face in its wake
will leave scars to match
my charred, disfigured soul.
and only then,
will you see me
for what I am.
only then,
will you run, screaming,
instead of longing
to lay next to me
in this bed.
you will not
be fooled
by me again.

fix

Never found pleasure in being used till you used me as a muse, lit a fuse, struck my heart and left a bruise.

And I'm weak and bleeding, helpless and pleading, till tables turn and I burn your skin, and you learn my sin, and you yearn for me, earning me back again.

Wild after dark, slut in a park, gasoline to my spark, strike, leave a mark. Mind races, breathless chases, hungry embraces, aching in places, stripped bare and tasted.

Lust drunk and beaten, ravaged and eaten, worshipped and weakened. Have me, hold me, bend me, fold me. Insatiably thirsty, begging for mercy. Heal me and hurt me. Praise me and curse me.

Women who want you plead while I taunt you. I know I haunt you. Recklessly referenced, pinned and defenceless, starving, relentless.

Ache while I take, break while I stake my claim on your lips. Say my name. I'm your fix.

read between the lines

I write when I'm unhappy.

Take that as you may in an attempt to psychoanalyse me.

My creativity wanes with the pain, and I must admit that at times, I miss the misery. The craving, longing, wanting parts of me that come to light after one too many a lonely night.

Yet the fantasies that once assumed control of me are now overtaken by blistering reality. Phantom kisses and balcony wishes are no more. Too many qualms to hold a wayward dream in my palms and while I miss the whirlwind of words within, it is refreshing to finally exhale silence in place of prose or poetry.

I am no longer the product of longing times hurting, gushing forth and covering the floorboards in the blood of my pen without warning.

And there is comfort in the quiet. A writer I may be, yet as much as I identify with it, there is more to me than beer and tear-stained pages and cigar-smoke nightmares on empty stages.

I find some semblance of stability in the stagnancy.

An acceptance of my own presence lingers in the humid room as waves of steam ascend from sunburnt limbs. No cries into the void or the night but a novel tranquility within.

And though I will attempt to mask his appearance to some degree, it is unlike me not to speak of my present tense with an unapologetic ease.

Yet, I needn't shout of him to the ends of the earth. I prefer to hold him deep within constricted arteries, for he may very well be the blood to sustain me, the fight over flight when confronted with unabashed honesty, the acceptance of easy alongside his complexities.

He may well possess hands worthy of covering my lips to stifle almost-screams. And I will savour the flavour of contentment in a place other than dreams. There are volumes to read between the lines I haven't been writing.

things that don't suck

A lazy Sunday afternoon spent in bed with the blinds drawn. The sound of rain pelting a tin roof. Skin on skin, pressed to him as his fingers move slowly through your hair. Firm hands massaging aching shoulders tirelessly, releasing months of pent-up tension. A raspberry sour ale at 7:40 a.m. after trudging in from a 12 hour night shift. Sinking into a scorching bubble bath, limbs melting, exhaling deeply. The warmth of August sunlight on exposed skin, face-down on a towel, hands resting on steaming sand. Catching a frog with your bare hands in the creek at the camp. Kisses on the jaw and neck. Driving too fast on a paved two-lane road with the wind rushing in. Sea salt and honey flavoured bacon. A snowstorm on Christmas Eve. Singing Bohemian Rhapsody with your cousins, crammed together on a piano bench. A big dog resting its head on your thigh. Tobogganing. Chris Stapleton or TJ Osborne singing anything. Men who work with their hands. Legs draped over his on the front porch at 1 a.m., tipsily spilling secrets. Clydesdales prancing in an open field. A crackling fireplace and fuzzy blankets. Arms to fall into after waking from a bad dream. Menthol cigarettes. Intense eye contact between kisses. Bookshops and empty libraries. Campfire serenades. A muse who reads your poetry. A newborn baby sleeping on your chest. Lemon meringue. Slow dancing in the moonlight. Sitting next to the river watching the rapids. Flexed forearms and biceps.

Strawberry shortcake. Solitary walks in the forest, listening to the birds sing. Pierogis and poutine. Hugs from your family. Handwritten messages. The ocean. Believing he's out there wondering what I'm like. Falling in love when the timing is right.

shiver

I imagine
falling into you,
dizzily resting
my head on your shoulder.
your face in my hair,
sigh escaping your lips,
fingers interlaced,
hearts in our throats,
clinging to a fleeting paradise,
our bodies screaming
'finally.'

as much as I like
to fantasize
about forceful arms,
raw skin
and sore lips,
it isn't that
that comes to mind
when I can't sleep at 3 a.m.
it's the sense
that you'd be
a safe harbour for me
after countless years
tossed around at sea.

it's the thought
of your hands,
feather-light,
tracing my scars
in the moonlight.
it's the way your smile
makes my skin flush
and my soul shiver.

the ache

I know the ache,
the formidable chasm
beneath your ribs
that cannot be patched.
the despair and hopelessness,
the frantic search
for anything to numb the searing pain,
the revolving door between
self-loathing and self-medication.
the questioning of purpose,
the worthlessness,
the hurt burning within us.
the desire to put an end to it –
the suffering becoming too much to take.
I know it too - the loneliness.
but I am with you
beneath the bedsheets,
despite every mile between us.
I am tracing your palms,
memorizing the pattern of them,
and my fingers are methodically
running through your hair
as your head rests, heavy in my lap.
I am soft lips whispering reminders
of how much you mean to me.

I am warmth and consistency
countering your uncertainty.
I am the overwhelming sensation
that words will never explain.
I am yours, mind and body,
and you need not ever
be strong around me,
because I am madly in love
with every jagged piece of you.

drunk again

this one's for you.
I lift the glass,
trace it along
my bottom lip,
close my eyes,
tip,
savour
the flavour
as it colours
my mouth red.
sour raspberry
blend of bliss,
sizzling,
crackling
like Pop Rocks
on my tongue.
I smile, wince,
imagining
you taste
something
like this.
drunk again,
dreaming
of you
on my lips.

if you can

for some time, you've pursued me
through a forest of vibrant foliage
crawling with dazzling creatures,
littered with an array of forked paths
leading to a plethora of destinations
that undoubtedly appear desirable
to a man with a faulty attention span.

and while you often lose sight of me,
you have this uncanny ability
to cover ground expeditiously,
and just when I begin to think
I have lost you entirely,
you call to me.

and the sound of my name
on your tongue causes me
to pause carefully
and glance back
at this mercurial man,
bright-eyed and panting.

and as much as I long for you
to walk this path alongside me,
I simply turn and carry on soberly.

we both know I stop for no one,
and I think you enjoy the idea
of travelling with me far more
than you would the reality.

but if ever you can, darling,
for the love of God,
catch me.

jonesing

you saw my mind
and raised your glass —
a rare understanding
between strangers.

we looked upon
our past lives,
the things we love,
the demons we conceal.

the openness,
the way you allow me
to bare myself
is addictive.

you accept all of me,
hearing whilst knowing,
parts of you mirrored
in my weary eyes.

jonesing for your presence,
thirsty for late-night musings,
inexplicably drawn
to every facet of your being.

inimitable, all-consuming —
your words soothe me,
your existence jars me
and shakes up all my atoms.

sharing cigarettes

chain-smoking on the porch,
slumped in a patio chair,
eyes on the starlit sky,
expelling breath in white wisps.

in the right company
or the wrong mindset,
I'll go on till the pack is gone.

savouring that familiar burn
on the roof of my mouth,
tension gradually dropping
with the temperature.

the lateness of the hour
or the harsh reminder
of winter gently whispers,

pulls me back in time
to long nights with you,
shivering, philosophizing,
bleeding out dreams and desires.

I come back to that
time and again, even as I sit
in deafening silence.

the trees are ominous, barren,
fallen leaves brown and shriveled,
the first snowfall dusts the ground,
fashioning small drifts of ivory powder.

it's artistic, nostalgic,
that I'm killing myself like this.
the thought of you is metastatic.

needing to be unhinged again
the way you permitted me to be.
craving the depth we had,
despite the promised tragedy.

filling our lungs and freezing our limbs
with little interest
in the warmth awaiting us inside.

spilling out darkness and swimming in it,
something more than kindred spirits.
our souls helplessly intertwined,
sharing cigarettes one bitter night.

say when

tilt my jaw and pour
liquor down my throat
like you mean it.
tangle your fingers
in my hair and lean in
to whisper promises
and lies in my ear,
as my lashes close slowly
and I sigh, wanting
so much more of this.
put your mouth on mine,
intoxicated together.
forget to remember
what you know about me.
kiss away the lonely.
make me whole again,
if only for a minute.
my hands on your body,
both measured and frantic.
slipping off your shirt
as you tear away mine,
skin on skin intertwined,
breathing erratic,
static electricity.
needing you closer —

behind me, beside me,
over and under me.
hold me, restrain me,
make me writhe beneath
the heat of your tongue,
legs shaking, face numb.
tease me, make me beg for it,
then give it to me slowly.
spine contorting,
clenched teeth.
know me from the inside.
strangled kisses,
mouths opening wide.
let your rhythm
play mercilessly
over and over again
until I say when.

flinch

Violent bolts of illumination traverse menacing midsummer skies forcibly. Miraculous apparitions emerging aglow, arising from immeasurable darkness and branding unsuspecting retinas with blinding foretold fortune. Lightning-laced digits trace acquiescent heavens, rearranging stars, designing unimaginable constellations and agitating astrology, rendering it relevant for the time being. Sonnets written in galactic ink cause imaginary deities to blink egotistically before continuing to ignore all creation once again. Resounding reverberation, stimulation of ossicular vibration. Tempestuous transduction, electric impulsivity propagating the potential of our adrenalizing union. Flashing and echoing, sight and sound, he and I; alight despite eternal night, causing even the earth itself to tremble and flinch at our intensity.

when I'm dead

spurting onto paper,
severed from my head,

will the words I stitch together
keep living when I'm dead?

crippled

don't write about me —
I mean it.
don't say something
for the sake
of me believing it.
you don't love me.
I don't love you.
we've been here before,
it's nothing new.
if we were closer
in distance,
we'd fuck
and accept it
as the end of it.
so don't try to capture
my bleeding heart —
it isn't worth it
to make me crave it
or wish I deserved it —
whatever sweet words
you let escape you,
we both know
they're far from true,
and I'd rather avoid you
than swallow a lie from you.
so don't chase it.

erase it
while you can.
because while you think
you have the upper hand,
I could take it anytime,
and you'd be mine
to destroy in time.
it doesn't end well
for either of us,
so leave us
where we started.
let me remain
brokenhearted.
don't breathe the words
I long to hear.
leave me crippled
like this, my dear.

light

Undress me. Strip me down slowly. Slowly. The world has been cold to me. I grew tired of unforgiving air on me. Tired of feeling. The layers cover me. Cover the heart of me. Cover that part of me that longs to be exposed and naked, aching. My jacket is the first to fall and when it hits the floor it rattles like metal. Armor becoming unbecoming. See me. Eyes gauging my reaction as you reach for the hem of my sweater. An assenting response as I lift my arms and the fabric slips overhead before it thuds to the ground like chainmail, heavy. My heart visibly fluttering beneath the layer remaining. And I don't mind if you have a knife. Cut me with whatever you're concealing and press it in deep. You make me feel light. Fingers in belt loops tug me against you, your hand clasps the back of my neck. Tilt my head and leave your tender kiss on my jawline, lips. Gravity is no match for me, feet lifting, levitating. Pants unzipped, sliding over feminine hips, bare legs lithe and scarred scratched feet revealing secrets, like I've always been running.

And without even opening, your mouth begs I stay at least the night and I am light. I am the balloon and you the string and as long as you hold me I will be here. Is that clear? And the t-shirt lifted and tossed aside reveals my body in all its scourged and beaten glory. And your hands grip my arms as you examine me closely.

Only bits of lace remain, though we both know this is only the beginning of the undressing. And I am floating, body yearning for the sky or ceiling but still you hold me. Don't let go or I will disappear up there and no earthly man will ever reach me again. You lay me on silken sheets and pinned beneath you I feel free for the first time since sometime before this life began. And slowly, slowly, your fingertips trace my face. Eyes closed, breathing fast, my lips part as your finger moves over them. And the plaster cracks and the mask begins to lift, composure slipping, tension dissolving, and these eyes no longer hide what I'm feeling. My gaze telling as you fall into the abyss of passionate agony that constantly consumes me. And you know me in ways even God never knew me.

And with every rousing kiss you plant on my body, I nurture a garden of blossoming certainty. And the fortress walls are crumbling, and the chokehold around my neck is lessening, and the heat of your breath melts the ice that formed gradually time and again as I was touched or assaulted by unworthy hands. Slowly... slowly. Shoulders fall naturally, dipping to the mattress, and you free the bindings tied around my chest. And I spill out for you like a flood, and my heart is a force to be reckoned with, and the light within me to anyone else would be blinding, but you are one with it.

Hand on my breast, feel the apical pulse of me, the molten blood rushing through me, the raging disaster of me. Hear the fire alarms and the sirens screaming. But there is no smoke here — only fire in a vessel under pressure. And the way you move with me as you regard me with reverence, daring me to unleash at once all my heat, is the remedy for the ailment destined to kill me.

And you will not fight the fire. You will let it fuel and consume you. And the walls and the bed are burning, and there are no more layers, and I cannot be tamed or covered. And with attentive hands and lingering lips, you are at peace in the depths of me, and you see me. You lay me bare and begging that you lose yourself over and over within me, and this is unlike anything my whirlwind mind ever dreamed imagining. Slowly. You see me, and I am light.

blind faith

I will no longer allow
my faith the opportunity
to become a fantasy.
thus far, my dreams
have not been good to me.
I believe in soulmates unfailingly.
I believe we all have many,
and some of us have the privilege
of loving one until our days' end.
I may imagine your touch
as I fall asleep lonely,
but I will not scrawl out
another false, hopeful prophecy.
I'll cross my fingers and heart
with the hope that you'll find me,
and until then I will keep
my faith in you as quiet
as I do my belief in a god above.
I will not scream for you,
or endeavor to make you appear
in a place you are not.
but I will know you exist
when the rain falls on my skin,
when the midday sun
warms my shivering limbs,
when the wind caresses me.

I will know you in the way
the river runs infinitely,
and on nights when it seems
all the stars are falling.
I needn't speak of you
to affirm my belief in you,
but I am waiting devoutly
to feel your lips silencing
the whispered prayer
lingering on mine.

truth and oxygen

I didn't ask to be
the moon, and you
did not anticipate
the tidal force of me.
drawn in so forcefully,
inexplicable gravity,
a subtle illumination
penetrating what presented
as insurmountable darkness.
and though I shone
boldly for the masses,
you saw me telescopically,
intently examining craters
when others only ever
saw the shape of me,
or basked in my light
without knowing me
intimately.

you are an ocean
of vast perplexity,
and many fall victim
to your violent tsunamis.

but my area of interest
lies beneath your surface,
and I scrawl obsessively
on chalkboards and napkins,
endeavoring to solve
your obtuse equations,
diving blindly to the depths
of your madness to scour
a sunken ship for treasure
they say is hidden in wreckage.

but with hasty ascent comes
decompression sickness,
and you leave me desperate
for truth and oxygen.

last night I noticed
your voice was different —
as if there was humility in it.
and you philosophized
while I listened, and when
you told me the moon
was framed by branches,

I stepped into midnight
to gaze up at the sky,
and for a moment,
the clouds were thick,
until as if on command
they parted, and when
that half-moon emerged,
I shivered, in awe of it.
and we both looked at it,
conscious of its significance,
closer in our distance.

the law of gravitation
is perfectly clear,
but I'm unsure who
is pulling who here.

solace

so it is and must be,
seeking solace at sea.
push me to my death.
drag me to the depths.
turbulent creature,
drawn to danger,
weakened and weary,
eternal battle ending
with ocean influx,
gasp and spasm.
surrendering to
an inescapable fate,
waves the hearse
carrying me away
to a distant shore.
and you will know
to find me there.
fall to your knees
and grasp sopping hair,
lift this heavy head,
graze translucent skin
with eager fingertips.

search for depth
in eyes, wide and fixed,
and smile with relief -
for the two of us
are now at peace.

hazy

on a scale of one to hold-me-all-night,
how lonely are my eyes?
you could break me,
and that's alright.
I hope you try
when the border
between us ceases
to exist, and I finally taste
your hazy IPA kiss, and you're
shivering beneath my lingering lips.

still

I wanted to believe
in the finality of that apology,
and you've distanced yourself
from my writing,
and I'm unsure now
if you're quietly wading
in the depths of my mind,
or if it was easy
for you to stop reading;
if it was too much
to be cognizant
of these incessant feelings.
and I thought
the hypothetical distance
had tempered my interest,
but I haven't figured out
how not to want you
when we're standing
in a room together.
I haven't found the antidote
for the butterflies
that swallow my soul
each time we lock eyes.
you're the right kind of high.

and she's lucky,
and I care for you enough
that I wish you happiness
regardless of my presence
in your life, but damn it...
if you ever find
yourself alone again,
know that my heart
would bleed
passion and romance.
know that I would hold you
like no one ever has.
know that I am here
in an otherwise empty bed,
trying not to yearn for you,
wishing I didn't feel
what I still feel for you,
wondering if when
we part ways you sit alone
in the dark for a moment,
thinking of me.

I know you may not be,
and I know you never
asked to be
the muse,

but here
we are,
still.

for rent

My heart is not for sale. Without fail, you saw the sign in the window that read 'For Rent'. Called me up and had to know the price. Didn't think twice when told what's included, even as I alluded to imperfections, you saw reflections of all the things you thought you needed.
Warning heeded - not cheap - in fact, rather steep, but more than worthwhile.

And I said, bring your baggage and I will hold it within my walls. Let me be that temporary place, saving grace, a safe place to land, that warm hand in yours, that four-poster bed, that place to lay your head after the worst day, that empty promise uttered, "you can always stay".

But don't ever call me home. We both know this ends in you and I alone. For I am eclectic, impractical and dramatic. I will indulge your bad habits. You will spill wine on my carpets and smoke in the bathtub and blare loud music until dawn. And I will endure your damages, for one day, you will be gone.

One day you will tire of these halls. One day you will abandon these crimson walls for a sunny kitchen. For marble countertops that glisten. For the sound of your children's laughter. For your happily ever after.

And I can't fault you for reading through this chapter, but tell me you'll remember your wild tenancy long after you abandon your boyish tendencies and leave me echoing your name, empty. When that day comes your memory will haunt me even after I clean the floors and open the doors to the next guest.

For I am never a home, but always a place to rest.

ABOUT THE AUTHOR

Lauren Radey lives along the St. Lawrence River in Ontario, Canada. By day, she works in the mental health field, and by night, she plays with words and works as an editor. She is an avid book and beer connoisseur and loves to play music.

Lauren draws poetic inspiration from her own struggles with anxiety and depression, from the picturesque landscapes that surround her, and from romance, sensuality and longing.

With an affinity for introspection, a wild imagination and a propensity for unapologetic honesty, Lauren seeks to expose the raw, unfiltered essence of self and humanity in her writings.

'Weak Without a Vice' is Lauren's first published collection of poetry and prose. More of her work can be found on Instagram via @written.by.lauren

index

mind control..7

spring fever..8

in the moonlight 10

in April 11

lioness 14

self-made grave...15

devotion..17

sahara..19

body language 20

autumn leaves...21

shotgun girl 23

lingering 24

worst case 26

lately 27

hopscotch..29

these hands 30

skeletons 31

ashes..32

I write to you..33

barstool chemistry	35
unchain me	36
an apology	37
men at work	39
toothpaste	41
dead flowers	42
older man	44
the moth and the spider	46
the madness	47
sick serenade	48
you and my imagination	50
broody man	52
all bad	53
rock and roll	54
tension and whiskey	56
a dream	57
instant gratification	59
remember together	62
breathe	64
everything	67

careless 69

sometime in September 70

as you wish 74

the devil herself 75

they call it falling 77

blue smoke 78

harsh reality 79

bloom 81

safe word stop sign 83

chasing ghosts 85

be the rain 87

over easy 88

bleeding out 90

precipice 91

in love with a poet 93

never 95

this feeling 97

the cynic 98

spiders 100

boston 102

when you know 103

a flood 104

I tried 106

all night 107

blunt force trauma 109

the ghost 111

melting 113

raw 114

tangled limbs and pounding hearts 117

secrets 119

waiting to break 121

sinking 122

shooting heroin(e) 123

love charade 127

expectations 128

broken-heart syndrome 130

drunk on you 132

reversed polarity 134

love, or the idea of it 136

drifting 138

blue velvet	139
Cardinal	140
dose increase	143
sex and cigarettes	144
lonely in love	145
friction	147
you, me	148
unapologetic	149
grappling	152
derailed	154
don't stop	155
rocket fuel	157
strange	159
circling the drain	160
a burning question	162
reckless	163
too	164
loving me is a death sentence	166
the muse	168
lightning	169

human	171
cigars and stiff drinks	173
carry on	174
the end	175
between the lines	178
bones	180
days like this	182
hardwired to hurt	183
the bridge	184
prison	186
ce soir	187
life sentence	188
capsized	189
pieces	191
falling	194
a spring that never comes	195
lingerie	197
who you could have been	200
in it	201
attraction to distraction	204

when you read me 205

drowning in Portland 207

the best part 210

careful 211

volcanic 212

weak without a vice 214

space 216

hard to break 217

in October 219

games 221

6:48 222

I'd love it 223

weak and complete 225

too much 227

what's meant to be 229

ecstasy 230

held inside 231

red-handed 233

before I lose myself 236

a poet's bed 238

glitch 239

lucky you 241

bloodthirsty..242

you win 243

cold-hearted 246

smoke rings (one night with you)..248

the long way home 251

possession 253

leave me dreaming..254

embers..256

growing pains 257

lakeside musings..259

the nerve 260

fragile mind..262

filthy...264

I tell the moon...265

on the beach alone 267

like the leaves..269

parallel lines 270

fluorescent wasteland 271

blind	273
trust issues	274
poets and pain	275
ethereal erythropoiesis	277
fault lines	279
free association	281
no mercy	283
don't	285
to know you	286
her	288
ode to dark roast	290
snack	291
lies	292
spilled	294
self-destruct	295
unwritten	297
please	298
delicate	300
the flowers	302
the whisper	304

made-up man	306
13	309
hanging	311
use me	312
the woman rides away	314
starlight	318
a quiet day	320
daily meds	321
plan b	323
fall	325
fusion	326
cedar and smoke	329
heliocentric heartache	330
(x)	331
not close enough	334
marbles	336
this breath	338
solutions	340
in the darkness	342
fooled	344

fix	345
read between the lines	346
things that don't suck	348
shiver	350
the ache	352
drunk again	354
if you can	355
jonesing	357
sharing cigarettes	359
say when	361
flinch	363
when I'm dead	364
crippled	365
light	367
blind faith	370
truth and oxygen	372
solace	375
hazy	377
still	378
for rent	381

about the author 384

index 387

Copyright © 2021

All rights reserved. No part of this publication may be reproduced, distributed, or transmitted in any form or by any means, without prior written permission, except in the case of brief quotations embodied in critical reviews and certain other non-commercial uses permitted by copyright law. This is a work of fiction. Names, characters, places, and incidents are a product of the author's imagination. Locales and Public Names are sometimes used for atmospheric purposes. Any resemblance to actual people, living or dead, or to businesses, companies, events, institutions, or locales, is completely coincidental. Contents are the author's works. All alterations have been subject to author consent and approval. Formatting and presentation have been completed with the author's preferences in mind.

Photography: Iris Laurencio
Editor: Nat White
Cover Design: Adric Ceneri / Nat White
Interior Format and Design: Nat White

ISBN: 979-8- 503-163-117 (Print Version)